Parents, Children, Teens, and Psychological Viewpoints on Parenting Practices in Kuwait and Greece

Parents, Children, Teens, and Psychological Viewpoints on Parenting Practices in Kuwait and Greece

Juliet Dinkha
With Nathasha S. Sharma
and Nourah Al Enezi

LEXINGTON BOOKS
Lanham • Boulder • New York • London

Published by Lexington Books
An imprint of The Rowman & Littlefield Publishing Group, Inc.
4501 Forbes Boulevard, Suite 200, Lanham, Maryland 20706
www.rowman.com

86-90 Paul Street, London EC2A 4NE

British Library Cataloguing in Publication Information Available

Library of Congress Cataloging-in-Publication Data

Names: Dinkha, Juliet, author. | Sharma, Nathasha S., author. | Al Enezi, Nourah, author.
  Title: Parents, children, teens, and psychological viewpoints on parenting practices in Kuwait and Greece / Juliet Dinkha, with Nathasha S. Sharma and Nourah Al Enezi.
  Description: Lanham : Lexington Books, [2023] | Includes bibliographical references and index.
  Identifiers: LCCN 2023002638 (print) | LCCN 2023002639 (ebook) | ISBN 9781666925074 (cloth) | ISBN 9781666925081 (ebook)
  Subjects: LCSH: Parenting--Kuwait. | Parenting--Greece. | Families--Kuwait. | Families--Greece. | Parenting--Psychological aspects.
  Classification: LCC HQ755.8 .D523 2023 (print) | LCC HQ755.8 (ebook) | DDC 306.87409495--dc23/eng/20230313
  LC record available at https://lccn.loc.gov/2023002638
  LC ebook record available at https://lccn.loc.gov/2023002639

Contents

Acknowledgments

"Writing a book is harder than I thought and more rewarding than I could have ever imagined. This is a feeling I had when I wrote my first book, and this feeling has only intensified the second time around. The idea of writing this book came as an extension of my first book *Navigating Social Identity: A Young Adult Story of Time,"* which focused predominantly on youth and young adults navigating through the formation of their social identity. This book further explores identity formation by integrating the effects of parental trauma on raising the "ideal" child.

First and foremost, I want to thank the American University of Kuwait (AUK) administrators for their support of my academic interest and scholarship. Dr. Rawda Awwad and Dr. Ali Charara, thank you for always believing in me and supporting my research without borders. I also would like to thank all my colleagues and administrative staff in the Department of Social and Behavioral Science at AUK for their support and encouragement. A big thanks to my family, especially my children Larson and Larsa who allowed me the time and space to complete this book. I am very appreciative of the support and patience that you both provided during my journey. I understand that my inability to always be emotionally available and my absences may have been unsettling at times. I also want to thank my supportive friends in both Kuwait and the USA—you know who you are—for putting up with my ongoing demands and requests for assistance. Your support, kindness and unconditional love made this journey easy. I would specifically like to thank James for his support when I needed it. You allowed me the space to be who I am and always tried to understand my frustration without judgment and for that, I am deeply appreciative. My great co-authors Nathasha and Nourah, thank you for never giving up, for your persistence, patience, and for giving our families a safe place to speak. This book would not have been possible without the honesty and openness of the families that volunteered to be a part of our research. Thank you for allowing us into your homes, allowing us access into your lives and allowing yourselves to be vulnerable. Lastly, thank you Lexington Books for believing in our research and our ability to produce a publication that fills a knowledge gap for our diverse communities in the Mediterranean region."

—Juliet Dinkha

"Writing this book has been an emotional, rewarding, meaningful and heart-felt experience. None of this would have been possible without the individuals and participants who provided us with the honor of sharing their stories and experiences. I would like to personally thank all the participants from Greece for their time, openness, patience, vulnerability, and fearlessness. It has been a true privilege to be a part of their world and learn from them. I would like to thank my parents, Sanjiivv and Priya, who have tirelessly supported me through challenges in my life and encouraged me to continue growing. I am eternally grateful for their unconditional belief in me and their wholehearted love for me. Additionally, I could not have gotten through this book without the continuous emotional and at times, practical support of my partner, Spyros, who has been my rock, grounding me in times of darkness, overwhelm, stress and anxiety. I will forever be thankful for his presence, kind words, jokes, warmth, understanding and for always being my biggest cheerleader. It goes without saying, I am so thankful to my co-authors, Dr. Juliet Dinkha and Nourah Al Enezi for their continuous hard work, collaboration, friendship, insights, and support throughout the years. It has been a unique experience working alongside them, one I would never trade. Finally, I would like to truly thank our publishing team whose understanding, diligence and incredibly supportive efforts have made this a smooth and enjoyable process. This has been an incredible experience, one I did not know I would have so early on in life, I am undyingly grateful to anyone who has been a part of this journey with all of us."

—Nathasha Sharma

"Being able to write and publish this book has been one of the most meaningful things I got to experience, I am so thankful to have embarked on this journey with my co-authors Dr. Juliet Dinkha and Nathasha Sharma; they have both helped me grow and learn while offering me so much support during my educational journey as well as guiding me through my anxieties and fears, I am truly thankful to have them as my role models in the field of psychology. I would also like to thank my family, friends and friends who have turned into family throughout the way, for their continuous support and love. Dania thank you for being my best friend throughout the 10+ years I've known you, you truly inspire me to be the best version of myself, I love you forever. My sister who has also cheered me on when I wanted to give up, Sarah thank you for believing in me when no one else did. I would like to thank The American University of Kuwait from where I got to meet the wonderful Dr. Juliet as well as providing me with the opportunity to have worked on this project. Finally, I would love to thank everyone who shared their stories and opened up to all of us as well as trusting us with their experiences, without you this book wouldn't have been possible."

—Nourah Al Enezi

Introduction

On a daily basis, we meet impressive young individuals with a lengthy list of achievements despite facing difficult and aversive experiences in life, making them in one way or the other, what we like to call "millionaires." In our quest to understand how countless millionaires are built, we take a look at the subjective human experience of parenting, childhood influences, trauma effects, coping mechanisms, generational impacts, successes and regrets. Our exploration incorporates personal accounts from individual interviews with parents and their children, or vice versa, sharing their story. Interviews took place through online platforms such as Zoom or Skype, an intriguing process is discussed with our own personal emotions of the process embedded as well, in investigating how individuals react to questions, the extent to which they would share intimate information about their personal life and delving into understanding how they are choosing to raise or aim to raise their child, our next generation. We link the stories gathered to psychological models, theories of trauma and coping responses. One of our initial investigative questions included the following: Is there an ideal way to raise a child where they turn out successful, or do different approaches work? What makes different types of parenting work well? What are some consequences of distressing parenting? Quite a lot of this is explored earlier on, through the literature provided and then is brought to life through the personal stories. Our aim is to provide a deeper insightful look into several life experiences, get a better understanding of child rearing practices with a culturally informed perspective, generational effects as well as overall outcomes. However, our main intention was to provide a space where individuals would be heard, express their choices freely, could relate to others and feel that they weren't alone in facing these experiences. Additionally, we propose readers of this text to view stories as each parent's subjective impression of what strategies led to their child's development, along with significant and influential literature in the field examining each experience independently.

For several decades now, we have heard about researchers continuously investigating parenting and child development to understand what works and what doesn't work. Nowadays, parenting can be considered a culture of its own, which has been studied through different dimensions, styles, practices and patterns too. These are all distinct to one another, specifically, parenting practices are behaviors that encourage children to be social, supporting academic successes, involve reinforcement and discipline, as well as promoting and modelling critical problem-solving to children. Interestingly, defining parenting itself can take two directions: a supporting role and/or a controlling one (Kuppens and Ceulemans, 2019). This might make sense in a very general manner since we have all experienced or witnessed parents who may be displaying the two different directions evidently, but we are going to take a closer look into what really occurs behind these different directions of parenting. It is imperative to note that secondary literature from Kuppens and Ceulemans (2019) is not fully comprehensive without examining prominent theories by Mary Ainsworth, John Bowlby, Erik Erickson, Diana Baumrind, and Ann Masten; this will be revealed in the following sections.

Firstly, the supportive position of parenting, simply put, refers to the emotional aspect between a parent and a child. This normally includes the parent's involvement, commitment, responsiveness, obtainability, acknowledgement, validation, and warmness towards their child. This aspect has positive effects on the child's development in terms of preventing mental illnesses, alcoholism, and even behavioral struggles (Kuppens and Ceulemans, 2019). This category of parenting is closely related with John Bowlby's attachment theory, which describes an individual's typical pattern from infancy onwards, of relating in close caregiving and receiving relationships with "attachment figures" who are frequently one's parents or caregivers providing a balance of appropriate sensitivity and responsiveness to the child's needs in order to promote well-being as well as survival (Bowlby, 1969; Ainsworth, Blehar, Waters and Wall, 2015). Bowlby refers to this person as the "mother figure", which is utilized to explain why many of our stories by parents are concentrated upon mothers. It should be noted that attachment is not limited to parent-child relationships and can occur in other types of interpersonal relationships as well (Ainsworth, Blehar, Waters and Wall, 2015). According to Bowlby (1969), attachment is described as an enduring psychological connection between human beings, and can be used interchangeably with terms like "affectional bonding" and "deep-rooted emotional connection", connecting it to the current subject of supportive parenting. The theory of attachment entails the child's faith in the attachment figure's behavior and readiness to serve as both a stable foundation from which one can freely explore the world and a safe space from which the child can receive support, security, comfort during difficult times while seeking and sustaining a specific amount of proximity to the attachment figure (Bowlby, 1969). For a developing child, exploring the environment also comprises of interactions with others and internal introspection. However, because caregivers range in their degrees of presence and receptivity, not all children attach to caregivers in the same way. Consequently, there have been significant recent advancements in the fields of individual differences in the organization of attachment behavior and varied experiences related to the diverse attachment patterns (Ainsworth, 1979). Further literature by Ainsworth (1979) classifies distinct attachment styles in three categories of secure, avoidant and anxious-resistant, the latter two are also known as insecure attachment.

Early research into the distinct attachment styles postulated that caregivers who were more sensitive in their responsiveness to a child's needs lead to a more secure attachment in the developing child (Ainsworth, 1979). Children who interact with unreliable and inaccessible caregivers will have an insecure bond with them (Ainsworth, 1979). The child's dependence on the attachment figure as a source of security ("secure base'") is what determines the quality of early attachment connections. It is suggested that this appropriate responsiveness leads the child to construct an inner representation of the caregiver being accessible, reliable, trustworthy and therefore, feels more security within the attachment relationship (Ainsworth, 1979). It is hypothesized that this warm attachment responsiveness enables the child to develop an internal working model of the caregiver as being available, reliable, and trustworthy and increases the child's sense of security in the attachment connection. With this secure attachment, protection and presence of the caregiver serving as a reliable foundation, the child is more receptive to stimuli that may ignite exploration of the external (others, the world) and internal realms (the self) and this is where core belief systems are formed (Ainsworth, 1979). Additionally, Bowlby explained internal working models as the way early attachment experiences impact individuals throughout their lives that influence one's feelings, thoughts, and conduct in close relationships (Bowlby, 1969; Sutton, 2019). These internal working models, which are absorbed throughout childhood, become the default way of processing experiences with how romantic relationships function, how caregivers behave, and how to resolve conflicts and communicate effectively (Sutton, 2019). According to research, parent-child interactions help organize numerous areas of a child's development, such as affect management, mental health, and interpersonal relationships. A number of familial experiences, especially parenting, structural changes in the family, family conflict, marital satisfaction, conflict resolution abilities, and even intimate partner abuse, are consistently linked to attachment in empirical studies (Sutton, 2019). Other outcomes like affect regulation, psychopathology, memory, and attentional processes have also been the subject of attachment theory applications in continuous studies (Sutton, 2019). Linking back with supportive parenting, the warmth, accessibility, attunement and involvement suggest it leads to secure attachment bonds with the child.

A major component of supportive parenting involves modeling or demonstrating to a child emotional self-regulation skills to cope with distress (that is, how to control oneself, manage challenges, communicate and process difficult emotions), promoting empathy for others and other compassionate/altruistic behaviors. It has been suggested that individual variations in affect regulation can be explained by attachment theory as well. The theory holds that while under stress, the attachment bond is triggered and children seek out attachment figures to reestablish security. This is made possible through seeking closeness to the caregiver. Children learn effective emotion regulation when caregivers are attentive to requests for proximity (Sutton, 2019). As we have seen above, emotional regulation rather than dysregulation is an impact of secure forms of attachment through early parental experiences demonstrating this. When children grow older, this type of parenting is important in not only molding them into upstanding members of society but also ensuring they are able to handle any practical or emotional obstacle they might face throughout their lives. As parents, our end goal is only to make sure that our children can be happy and live fulfilling lives, and often, we serve as their models showing them what that looks like as well.

The other direction that parenting takes is controlling, which means parents manage psychological and behavioral dimensions of a child's development with force. We have all probably heard or seen parenting through behavioral control several times in our lives. Oftentimes, it is embedded in our culture and how the previous generations (i.e., our parents and their parents) thought of parenting. Due to this, we learned consciously or unconsciously that this is what parenting looks like and whether we choose to or not, we may repeat such parenting behavior with our children. Controlling parenting resembles handling or managing children's behaviors by implementing demands, rules, discipline/corrective schemes, monitoring their rewards and punishments. Let's not completely discount control, as humans, we need a little bit of control in our lives to feel stable and secure. The same goes for parenting, research has shown that a certain amount of parental control is seen as a positive influence on development through structure, routine, and repetitive learning (Kuppens and Ceulemans, 2019). However, what becomes damaging is the use of excessive control such as physical punishment (e.g., hitting/spanking). These aspects of physical punishment are considered traumatic to the small fragile brains of children who do not always understand adult reasoning as to why their parents may do this and only remember the pain of the experience throughout life. In fact, research has linked physical punishment to stored traumatic experiences across development and this is explored further in our next chapter. Likewise, deficient control such as lack of attention, supervising and engagement with a child has been linked to the rise of mental health concerns like depression, anxiety and misbehavior.

Controlling parenting, as discussed above can take a behavioral role as physical punishment but it can also take on a psychological role of control as well. Psychological parental control involves intrusive control or influence over the child's mind and mental world such as their thoughts, feelings and beliefs (Tian et al., 2019). Sometimes this can look like devaluing a child, using guilt to force them into doing something or withdrawal of affection towards them (Tian et al., 2019). This type of parenting, especially combined with behavioral control, leads to consequences such as depression, anxiety, deviancy, increased aggression and other mental health concerns (Kuppens and Ceulemans, 2019; Tian et al., 2019). Psychological control is often a deeper source of trauma influencing a child's autonomy and authenticity about oneself, the world and others. The effects of this sort of control can last all the way into adulthood and much longer too. When controlling parenting is used, attachment insecurity may occur due to the unpredictability and unreliability of parental figures to provide security. Maltreatment and violence in the family are two of the most researched risk factors for the emergence of insecure attachment (Sutton, 2019). One may assume that those who are raised by abusive parents would have an insecure attachment style since they regard their parents as unsupportive, unresponsive, dismissive, and hostile. Based on a recent meta-analysis involving young children, children who had experienced abuse had 80% higher odds of having an insecure attachment style than children who had not (Sutton, 2019). Importantly, current research confirms that childhood neglect, emotional abuse, verbal abuse, sexual abuse and physical abuse are all linked to the development of an insecure attachment style in both adolescence and adulthood, either through an anxious or avoidant attachment style (Sutton, 2019). Moreover, Ainsworth, Blehar, Waters and Wall (2015) note in their 'Strange Situation' study that children whose attachment figures have ignored their needs or had a delay in responsiveness or responded in an egregiously insensitive manner, learned that the caregiver is inaccessible or unresponsive. Consequently, the child may be more anxious and apprehensive of caregivers as they are unsure of what to expect, this lack of stability in the attachment figures behavior is said to lead to an insecure anxious attachment (Ainsworth, 1979). In this study, Ainsworth (1979) also suggests that caregivers who displayed rejection, anger and had greater restrictions on how they expressed emotions lead children to be more avoidant. Children who encounter inadequate parenting learn that seeking intimacy is a hopeless method of relieving their distress; as a result, these children develop secondary attachment techniques that they use well into adulthood (Sutton, 2019). For instance, when faced with potentially threatening or distressing situations, avoidantly attached individuals use detaching or dissociative techniques to block out their thoughts and feelings, inevitably avoiding the experience. Theoretically, these methods emerge when parents reject and forbid emotional expression without providing examples of effective emotion regulation (Sutton, 2019). Whereas, individuals with anxious attachments use hyperactivating coping mechanisms to constantly scan their surroundings for threat (hypervigilance), are more likely to spot danger in everyday situations and are unable to manage emotions. According to studies, these strategies appear when parents are intrusive and inconsistent to the extent that a child is unable to learn self-regulation abilities, as seen with controlling forms of parenting (Sutton, 2019). For instance, mothers who provided emotional support and guidance to their children had children with higher levels of secure attachment, whereas mothers who were dismissive of their children's emotions had children with lower levels of secure attachment. These results demonstrate the dyadic nature of attachment and emotion control. Data has also shown that although insecure individuals struggle controlling their emotions, secure people are successful at doing so. Due to a history of stressful situations and interpersonal interactions marked by rejection and inconsistent behavior, insecure individuals lack the mental stability to handle adverse life events (Sutton, 2019). Alcohol, anxiety, depression, and drug use issues are also more likely to occur in people with an insecure attachment style. There is a risk of aggression difficulties in both avoidant and anxiously attached children, corroborating similar impacts in controlling as well as abusive forms of parenting (Sutton, 2019).

We can link psychological parental control to aspects of Karen Horney's research on a child's need for safety and security which plays a crucial role in attachment as we have already examined in-depth and personality development. She proposes an interesting concept discussing the parent-child relationship in that, forced fear put onto a child tends to spill onto other aspects of development and the life cycle (Schultz, D. P., & Schultz, S. E. p.139). As an example, let's consider a common practice we all have heard of, where parents enforce certain career paths on children. This can push a child to develop fearful beliefs of not being worthy if they do not follow along and can damage the child's appropriate development of independence. Similarly, according to Erik Erikson (1963, 1968), social factors that affect human development play an important role in determining the identity of an individual's personality. Erikson maintains that from birth to old age, every child experiences a number of developmental periods, 8 stages in particular. Erikson (1963, 1968) highlighted adaptability that is based on cultural and historical context. His focal points of identity and intimacy for adolescence and early adulthood derive a significant portion of their meaning from the historical and cultural settings in which they are produced and articulated (Pittman et al., 2011). These included the dichotomy of 1) fundamental trust versus mistrust in infancy, 2) autonomy versus shame in toddlerhood, 3) initiative vs. guilt in early childhood, 4) industry versus inferiority in preadolescence and late childhood, 5) identity versus confusion for the adolescent years, 6) intimacy versus isolation in young adulthood, 7) generativity versus stagnation in adulthood, and 8) integrity versus despair in old age (Erikson, 1963, 1968; Erickson and Erikson, 1998). Each stage's goal was to eliminate the dichotomous conflict that defined the time period. However, nobody's experience during the course of a full stage of development is totally favorable or unfavorable, thus resolutions cannot be wholly negative or positive (Pittman et al., 2011).

Additionally, when the constructive part of the dichotomy was more prominent in the resolution, it would become clear that the psychological growth was progressing healthily. Early resolutions served as a springboard for future encounters, but those early resolutions might also be revised by subsequent experiences (Erikson, 1963, 1968; Erickson and Erikson, 1998; Pittman et al., 2011). The first four stages lay a basis for the latter stages and demonstrate how social and psychological processes are intertwined, which Erikson thought was essential to psychosocial progression. Early relationships between caregivers and children have a direct impact on the social aspect of psychosocial development (Erikson, 1963, 1968; Erickson and Erikson, 1998; Pittman et al., 2011). As a result, the degree to which the primary caregiver responds to the child's needs will determine how the basic trust-versus-mistrust dichotomy is resolved. Similar to Bowlby-Ainsworth's attachment theory where responsiveness and availability is vital for a secure attachment and the formation of basic trust with the primary attachment figure. Children whose development was observed by capable and loving caregivers may develop skills in relating, cooperating, and engaging with a constantly expanding network of meaningful individuals as they grow. Erikson argued that even as children's social connections widen, parents still have a crucial role to play (Erikson, 1963, 1968; Erickson and Erikson, 1998; Pittman et al., 2011). Optimal development is associated with active exploration and engagement with the outside environment across development. Children experiment with new ways of acting, knowing, and feeling with each stage as a result of their own developing interests and activities. Parents support this inquiry by offering opportunity, guidance, and help when difficulties arise, aiding once again in self- regulation (Pittman et al., 2011). These discoveries yield a lot of self-relevant information in the shape of experiences and social feedback (Pittman et al., 2011). For instance, understanding that school-aged children may be constrained in their ability to "assist" at home, a parent of a child in the initiative-versus-guilt phase may create options or opportunities and celebrate the effort the children display as they seek to complete the task. This may maintain a secure attachment by attuning to the child's needs at different stages and promote a supportive parenting stance. However, another parent may forbid, ridicule or punish the child, this could make the child feel guilty about their eagerness. If these parental signals are regularly communicated to the children in these two homes, it is not impossible to understand that the two children may learn completely distinct messages about themselves and their importance in the family unit (Pittman et al., 2011). This example demonstrates the extent of dynamic resolutions that can arise as the child and caregivers engage during a variety of everyday occurrences, comparable and interrelated to the formation of attachment.

Thus, excessive parental control can lead to consequences with mental health, especially in societies and cultures where mental wellness and illness are largely stigmatized making the child feel helpless and hopeless; this is especially prevalent in most of the Middle Eastern region. Bornstein (2012) mentions that culturally influenced parenting practices are based on needs, settings and beliefs surrounding each society. So, if we take a step back, are parental demands put on children a method of ensuring their survival as a group? Perhaps, this is how each belief was formed as a way of helping each member of the group have a valuable purpose, however, over the years, society and the world has changed so much that some cultural beliefs and rules may no longer be functional to younger generations. Perhaps, in the 21st century, these old practices are bringing out adverse effects presently. Through our journey, we touch upon reasons parents bring up their unfulfilled dreams and goals, impose it on their children who then end up carrying it out. We listened and dug through the reality of why many children are burned out, depressed, and may not have a great relationship with their parents due to stored traumatic experiences based on parenting practices. As we will explore soon enough, childhood or developmental trauma is linked to home life and family attachments based on early experiences which shape how we experience the world in the future through thoughts, behaviors and feelings.

We often quote several parenting styles in everyday conversation, but little do we know that those words we use without thinking much of are actually based on research. In the realm of parenting research, Dianna Baumrind (1967; 2005) is frequently cited as a forerunner. She created a typology with 3 parenting styles—authoritarian, authoritative, and permissive—to reflect disparities in typical parental behaviors. Parents' responsiveness and demandingness are often the two polarization factors that emerge from their behavior and practices that help explain the three styles mentioned above (Baumrind, 1996; 2005). In order to encourage individuality and self-assertion in their children, parents must be attentive to, supportive of, and obedient to their wishes. This is referred to as responsiveness, and it includes tenderness, independence, support, and meaningful communication. Demandingness is the assertion made by parents that their children must assimilate into the community through behavior management, confrontation, maturity demands, and surveillance of their activities (monitoring) (Baumrind, 2005). That being said, parental support, communication that fosters introspection, and psychological control change how behavioral control and monitoring manifest and impact children's development. This will sound very similar to Kuppens and Ceulemans' (2019) dimensions of parental support and control, which are comparable but not the same. However, in the interpretation of our stories, Baumrind's typology along with Kuppens and Ceulemans' literature will often accompany each other.

Baumrind (1971) proposed that authoritarian parents attempt to forcefully influence, manage, and assess their childrens' conduct based on a fixed set of rules. While permissive parents are slightly more tender, offering increase in autonomy rather than control. She claims that the authoritative parenting approach lies in the middle of the previous two polarities (Baumrind, 1971). This is when parents have significant, but realistic and logical expectations of their child's behavior, appropriately communicate, display warmth and attentiveness and implement a reason based approach rather than compulsion to direct their behavior. This type of parenting encourages children to make errors that they can learn from while remaining non-obtrusive and showing interest in their pursuit (Baumrind, 1971; Kuppens and Ceulemans, 2019).

Baumrind's typology and parenting elements were expanded by Maccoby and Martin (1983) some years later. They identified four parenting styles based on the combination of two dimensions: demandingness and responsiveness; authoritative (high in demand and responsiveness); authoritarian (high demand and low responsiveness); permissive (low demand and high responsiveness) and neglectful (low demand and low responsiveness) (Maccoby and Martin, 1983). On the other hand, Baumrind (1967, 1971, 2005) has extensively investigated the link between parenting practices and developmental advancement. Authoritarian and permissive parenting were linked to less desirable developmental results for children, whereas negligent parenting resulted in the worst outcomes for children (Kuppens and Ceulemans, 2019). This work repeatedly demonstrated that youth of authoritative parents had the most significant development outcomes. Other researchers have confirmed the aforementioned correlations. School performance and psychosocial skills in children, including maturity, resiliency, autonomy, and self-esteem, have repeatedly been linked to an authoritative parenting style (Kuppens and Ceulemans, 2019). Research on permissive/indulgent parenting shows associations with both internal (such as anxiety, depression, detached behavior, psychosomatic symptoms) and external (such as academic misconduct, delinquency, problematic coping), as well as with interpersonal skills, self-esteem, and problem solving. Negative developmental effects, such as hostility, conduct problems, psychosomatic symptoms, dissociation, and anxiety have consistently been linked to an authoritarian parenting style (Kuppens and Ceulemans, 2019). Neglected children had the worst outcomes across a variety of areas, including poor self-regulation as well as control and civic responsibility, low autonomy, antisocial traits, depression, anxiety, psychosomatic complaints and poor academic performance (Kuppens and Ceulemans, 2019). It is important to state that child neglect is also considered a form of trauma, along with physical and psychological control, this will be discussed in more depth in the next section on Trauma. Although each of these styles are quite distinct and on separate ends of a spectrum, only one reveals positive outcomes on child development, especially in white, middle-class families according to Baumrind's (1967) initial study.

However, research in other cultures have shown that extreme authoritarian parenting is used as a necessity to maintain social order, especially in countries with low socio-economic status (Bornstein and Bornstein, 2007; Smetana, 2017). Through this, we wanted to emphasize once again how cultural and ethnic discrepancies are vital factors to account for when taking a closer look into parenting styles and practices. Throughout this book, parenting styles and practices will become more familiar and life-like as you hear the collection of stories from individuals discussing how they experienced them. Although this book explores parenting in a subjective and unique perspective of each individual, we are able to link them to past research when dissecting evident parenting patterns. Also, apart from emphasizing culture, we also want to point out generational differences that play a huge role on different parenting practices and styles. The collection of stories encapsulates views of different generations embodying how parenting has changed or not across the following generations: Baby Boomers (1946–1964, post WW2), Generation X (1965–1980) and Generation Y or Millennials (1981–1996) (Kasasa, 2021).

Before we bombard you with another series of past literature that gives us more insight into various topics to come, let's quickly discuss the aim of this book and our exploration into this topic. We wanted to discover the differences and similarities of raising the 'ideal' child and consequences/outcomes of each of these from a personal, unique and subjective view of individuals, through their own voices. Rather than doing a study that basically discussed a topic we can all relate to in a broad scientific manner, we wanted to write a book through your voice, the experience of everyday individuals, the human account telling a story that we can connect with personally and through research too. Many themes that are discussed are quite sensitive and painful topics for most individuals, but this is a part of discussing the raw truth of parenting and childhood. It is important to emphasize that this book is an ethnography encompassing each individuals' successes and insights as parents and children, for the next generation, not a guide or critique of any sort but a source of information to ponder over. This research was based on interviews and active participation of the parents with the interviewer. This study is culturally based and does not follow the typical western view of interviews in research. We developed a trusting relationship with the parents as well as children, and embraced participation instead of research neutrality. All participants in this book are of different socioeconomic classes, ethnicities and backgrounds, sharing hopes, struggles, and reflections in understanding mental health and their children.

So, we wish to ask you to ponder for a minute, ask yourself, if there is a real recipe for raising a perfect or ideal child? Wait, what does a perfect or ideal child even mean? What does that look like? What does that entail? Does it actually work out? Since you know by now that parenting is culturally influenced, are parenting practices or even styles passed down from generation to generation identical as if they mimicked or altered every time or changed entirely? What factors play a role here? Can you think about yourself, your parenting practices or future parenting practices, your own parent's practices? Those are just a few thoughts to get you thinking for now.

Chapter 1

Trauma

Let's begin by pointing out right away that mental wellbeing is imperative for the general health and development of each individual. There is no debate about it, our brain is an organ just like any other and its health is important for life. With that being said, trauma and abuse at all ages, especially childhood experiences can take a toll on our mental wellbeing. Putnam (2006) states that an abundance of research connects early childhood abuse and neglect with severe continuous life struggles such as depression, suicide, substance abuse and medical issues as well (e.g., cardiovascular issues, cancer, diabetes). From 2006 to 2021, these facts have exacerbated causing a mental health epidemic. After experiencing so closely a physical health pandemic with COVID-19, you can definitely understand the alarm we might feel knowing that a psychological health epidemic threatens our most important tool for survival, our mind. Mental illness, very literally, alters our brain and body progressively over time, leading to daily life consequences (Hayes, 2015).

Evidently, especially during childhood, we may face Adverse Childhood Experiences (ACE's) which are: traumatic events that have negative, long-lasting effects on health and behavior (such as physical abuse, emotional abuse, neglect, sexual abuse, witnessing abuse of another person/domestic violence, family members who are substance abusers, family members who suffer from mental illness or suicidal attempts, death of a parent or incarceration of a loved one etc.) (Felitti et al., 1998). These experiences alter the course of a child's development, physically altering their brain from a healthy one to a more vulnerable one. Being exposed to ACEs is detrimental to children as they are unable to learn how to manage their emotions and thoughts, as well as being unable to relax their bodies, leading to higher rates of diseases and growing rates of addictions as a self-soothing mechanism (Felitti et al., 1998). Other psychological consequences include Post-Traumatic Stress Disorder (PTSD), increased depressive and anxiety symptoms, regressive behaviors (e.g., bed wetting), sexually inappropriate behaviors, suicidal tendencies, and behavioral disorders (Cohen & Mannarino, 2008; Jaberghaderi et al., 2004). Research has uncovered that child sexual abuse, physical violence or domestic abuse impacts up to 25% of children across the globe with conceivably severe and negative effects continuing into adolescents and adulthood, if untreated (Cohen & Mannarino, 2008). Contrary to physical or sexual abuse, which can be incident-specific, neglect frequently includes persistent circumstances that are harder to pinpoint than particular incidents (Hildyard and Wolfe, 2002). The absence of adequate care, responsibility, and protection for a child in relation to his or her age and basic needs is known as neglect. According to the World Health Organization (WHO 1999), neglect occurs when a parent fails to provide for a child's growth in one or more of the following areas when they are able to do so: health, education, emotional development, nutrition, shelter, and safe living conditions. As a result, neglect can only take place when the family or the caregiver has access to resources (Avdibegovi and Brki, 2020). The most prevalent type of child neglect in American studies—which accounts for roughly 50% of the instances that were looked into—involves inadequate supervision of a child, resulting in physical harm. The bulk of other cases of neglect involve physical neglect (i.e., failing to appropriately satisfy children's bodily requirements such as food, water, clothing), enabling illegal activity, abandonment, and educational neglect. Less frequently, though, cases involve medical neglect, failing in supervision resulting in sexual abuse, and failing to provide a child with the required medical treatments and/or poor hygiene (Hildyard and Wolfe, 2002). It is challenging to operationally define emotional neglect and being exposed to familial violence because they don't result in observable harm and frequently have a delayed effect on development. Emotional neglect can be understood as actions or inactions by the caregiver that may result in the child developing behavioral, affective, or mental disorders (Hildyard and Wolfe, 2002). According to estimates by Avdibegović and Brkić (2020), the incidence of child neglect ranges from 16.3% for physical neglect and 18.4% for emotional neglect up to 20.6% and 29.4% depending on age. Physical, affective, cognitive, and interpersonal development all evolve across the years from infancy to adulthood. The fulfillment of basic needs including proper nourishment, affective support, hygiene, physical as well as mental health services, mental stimulation, family dynamics, and secure living standards are among the many aspects that influence a child's growth and development. Development of a child is also seen through brain maturation as the brain grows significantly during the first few years of life (Avdibegovi and Brki, 2020). This growth is chronological and systematic, arranging the development of brain processes from the simplest to the most sophisticated functions. Deprivation caused by neglect can impede healthy necessary development and result in neural dysregulation and neurocognitive deficits (Avdibegovi and Brki, 2020). The brain regions in neglected children that control thought and emotion are frequently underdeveloped. The combination of neglect and other forms of maltreatment causes the brain's survival-related regions to grow excessively, which causes anxiety, impulsivity, lack of emotional regulation, and hyperactivity. Meanwhile, limbic and cortical processes remain underdeveloped, which has an impact on empathy and cognitive capabilities. Early childhood neglect, particularly prenatal neglect, has an impact on the size and functionality of the developing brain (Avdibegovi and Brki, 2020). Children that were neglected at a young age struggle with mental, linguistic, moral, emotional and behavioral processes. The emergence of behavioral issues in later life is significantly influenced by the expressive, responsive, and general vocabulary/linguistic developmental delays, linked to neglect (Avdibegovi and Brki, 2020). Children have substantial cognitive deficits, are more docile, distant, apathetic, participate very little in their social and physical environments and exhibit helplessness when distressed. It is suggested that the child internalizes the idea or belief that they are unworthy and expects to fail to make friends, achieve academically, or receive attention (Avdibegovi and Brki, 2020). A persistently negative self-perception, unfavorable interpersonal expectations, challenges in resolving interpersonal conflicts, and challenges in succeeding academically are all consequences of neglecting school-age children as well. According to Avdibegovi and Brki (2020), childhood neglect increases the likelihood of personality disorders, anxiety and depressive symptoms in adolescence, and the appearance of suicide and self-harming activities. Childhood maltreatment is linked to mental health issues in adulthood, including depression, PTSD, anxiety disorders, suicidal thoughts, drug misuse, and other risk-taking behaviors. Long-term physiological effects of neglect can include hypertension and chronic pain syndrome. The fact that parents of neglected children were frequently neglected themselves suggests that parenting practices are passed down through generations (Avdibegovi and Brki, 2020). Similar to studies of abused children, neglected children are more likely than non-neglected children to have anxious (i.e., insecure) attachments to their caregivers and later in life as we examined in the previous chapter (Hildyard and Wolfe, 2002).

Understandably, governments are rising up and beginning to address the growing rates of young individuals experiencing traumatic experiences, offering aid to help remedy or hinder long term negative effects (Hayes, 2015). Within the realm of psychology and mental health, there are a growing numbers of approaches and evidence-based interventions for children and families fostering growth, healthy development and providing tools for coping following traumatic experiences (e.g., Trauma Focused CBT). Based on all the information we just mentioned, it is evident now, how crucial it is to trace back and fully understand the impact of trauma, as well as, it's costs on emotional and behavioral elements in children (Cohen, Mannarino & Knudsen, 2005; Deblinger et al., 2011)

Let's begin with Albert Ellis (1913–2007), who is considered the father of the Rational Emotive Behavior Therapy (REBT) and acclaimed for the ABC model. The ABC model is quite simple to understand, Ellis uses A to represent external environmental events, B to represent our cognitions/thoughts, and C representing emotions and behaviors. Through this, we observe that A, B and C are linked to each other and affect each other. Ellis states that, we experience activating events (A) every day that prompt us to think about what is happening. The interpretation of these events results in the emergence of specific beliefs (B) about the event and our roles in the events. Once the belief is established, we experience the emotional consequence (C). Consider this example, our boss at work tells us that a task we did needs some alterations, this is the activating event (A), we then think about what we were just told and may think "I should have worked harder, I can't do anything correctly, I am not good at my job," these are the specific beliefs about the event and ourselves (B). Finally, we may experience emotions such as anger, sadness, overwhelming anxiety, dread and pressure which is the emotional outcome (C) of the event and our beliefs of it. This theory beautifully demonstrates how our beliefs about an event can help determine our response and therefore, the outcome. If our beliefs are rational, they lead to moderate emotions that allow us to act constructively. On the other hand, our irrational beliefs, which we have more often than not, lead to challenging emotions such as aggression, anxiety, or depression, that hinder us from achieving goals (Opre & Opre, 2006). Taking this into account, we can link here how experiencing physical abuse by a parent when a child does something wrong (A), causes a child to develop beliefs that they are 'not loveable, not good enough, defective etc.' (B) leading to emotional consequences such as depression, self-esteem issues, anxiety, PTSD and several others based on this one traumatic experience (C). If the child experiences several adverse experiences, the outcome can be just as severe.

Linking to theories discussing Trauma, they suggest that the development of emotional and behavioral issues can be separated into three subsections: Emotional, Behavioral and Cognitive difficulties. Emotional or Affective problems involve sentiments of unhappiness, fear, angst or anger. With children, some may develop extreme moodiness or difficulty in controlling/regulating their moods and emotions, usually known as Affective Dysregulation (Cohen & Mannarino, 2008). They also experience behavioral issues such as avoidance of trauma reminders (a place, person, thing or circumstance that may trigger the recollection of said trauma), this can also look like being distant from the person who has caused them harm. As a result, following the traumatic experience, children and adolescents can develop new oppositional behaviors and may feel emotions of betrayal in response to the injustice of the traumatic experience (Cohen & Mannarino, 2008). In simpler terms, children may think that the experience that they had to go through was unfair, unjust, wrong, and feel betrayed by the person who caused them such thoughts and harm. They may even develop new difficulties, especially when separated or isolated from adults (i.e., refusing to attend school, needing to sleep beside parents), regressive acts (i.e., thumb sucking, bed wetting) or other displaying signs of intense distress. Among adolescents, substance abuse is a common coping mechanism to avoid recalling the trauma or to manage emotional distress (Cohen & Mannarino, 2008). Cognitive difficulties may include inaccurate thoughts regarding why the traumatic incident occurred, who was to blame (oftentimes, blaming themselves for it), disgrace, shame or worthlessness as well as losing trust in others (Cohen & Mannarino, 2008). Children who blame themselves for what occurred and feel they are worthless of being loved or having positive things may start to act in self-destructive ways. For instance, befriending troublesome friends, skipping school, using drugs and/ or being hypersexual (Cohen & Mannarino, 2008).

What's more interesting is that neuroscientific studies have mentioned that the results of abuse and trauma either through physical, verbal or emotional abuse (e.g., neglect) all show similar brain alterations compared to children who have not experienced abuse at all (Nemeroff, 2016). What's important from this neuroscientific data is that the neural response centers in the amygdala—identified with controlling behaviors, impulses and emotional regulation—show increased reactivity in children exposed to trauma during early years of life. As we have discussed previously, behavioral, cognitive and emotions/affective consequences are the result of this and this evidently shows us the very literal biological change that occurs and goes unnoticed. Abused children have been found to have anomalies in stress hormone levels identified with dysregulation, heightened resting and receptive heart rate, blood pressure, and changes in immune functioning too (Cohen et al., 2004; Cohen, Mannarino & Knudsen, 2005). It isn't just our brain that changes when we experience trauma, but our entire body and our way of being/living is altered. However, we do not focus on the neuroscientific and biological aspect of trauma much, as this is not the focus of the current exploration. But what seems evident at this point, trauma and brain alteration result from environmental experiences that influences the make-up of an individual's insight, feelings, and character continuing long after the event has passed. Ellis's ABC theory fits in well here to help us grasp the deep impact of each traumatic experience on our entire existence and our children's.

But, there are some factors that protect us and build resilience when trauma or difficulties are experienced. Research points out that positive parent-child relationships, relations to other family and larger systems influence the extent of social wellness a child displays, as well as the level of resilience demon-strated during experiences of distress or trauma (Chen et al., 2012). As we delve into understanding the importance of these relationships, we will do so with a focus on the attachment theory when discussing trauma as well (i.e., bonds formed between infants and parents in the first years of life that teaches them about the world, others and themselves) and investigating how early experiences affect future behaviors and beliefs. Through the attachment lens, we see that evolution has ensured that when infants experience any feelings of distress, anxiety or fear, they immediately seek closeness to an adult who provides them with protection, care and comfort. When a child is triggered with experiences of physical discomfort, feelings of fear and danger (either physically, psychologically or emotionally), they seek comfort and security from their parents to soothe and relax them (Howe and Fearnley, 1999). If, however, the parent fails to offer comfort, protection or understanding, the child experiences prolonged periods of unregulated emotional distress. So, when there is a lack of sensitivity or concern from a parent during times of distress, the child internally learns that the parent is emotionally unavailable (Howe and Fearnley, 1999). This is a psychological loss of the parent, which further raises levels of distress and emotional stimulation in a child. These children begin to experience themselves as insufficiently worthy to warrant attention, love, comfort, understanding or protection leaving them with inse-cure beliefs repeating as a pattern throughout life (Howe and Fearnley, 1999; Finzi et al., 2001). In the ABC theory, we looked at how this would be the cognition/belief aspect which is affected by the parent's response to the child and is how our deepest core beliefs are formed and activated unconsciously throughout life.

There are two kinds of parent-triggered distress in insecure attachments linked to trauma. Either children are afraid of parents who physically abuse them or children are afraid of parents who are psychologically unavailable or unresponsive due to their own mental illness or unresolved trauma's (Howe and Fearnley, 1999). In both cases, the relationship with the parent is the source of fear and distress causing the rejected child to be overwhelmed with feelings of helplessness, hopelessness, vulnerability, loneliness and abandon-ment (Finzi et al., 2001; Howe and Fearnley, 1999). In return, this feeling of vulnerability is flooded by pain, anger, distress, dysregulation and feeling out of control. Linking once again to the ABC theory, these feelings then become (C), the emotional outcome of the belief and event. Likewise, children who received unpredictable parenting during childhood develop insecure attach-ments too and as adults they display exaggerated responses to distress such as hyperactivation (e.g., excessive anxiety and irrational view of oneself) or deactivation (e.g., avoidance to any distress by means of repression, distrac-tion or detachment) (Sharma, 2021). Insecure attachments, simply put, are brains that developed in survival mode. On the other hand, when a child has a well-connected positive relationship with their parents, where they receive support, security, nurturance and safety, their brain is equipped to form secure attachments. Their brains go through the appropriate development to ensure resilience is built to cope with adversity throughout life and this is how relationships serve as a protective barrier when dealing with obstacles. Then, children are able to sustain long term relationships later in life, are less likely to become substance abusers, display better life satisfaction and general overall well-being. That was definitely a lot to take in and reflect about. Feel free to take a few moments here to think about your responses and how this may apply to you, your loved ones or your children.

When examining trauma, it is quite important to discuss its effects on memory after a traumatic event, the focal point of numerous research studies across the last few decades. We may not know it, but memory can be explicit or implicit. Explicit memory is our conscious longer-term memory that functions based on an existing framework of previous experiences, factual semantic/narrative information and the integration of new experiences and events into it (Van der kolk, 1994). This resembles a modern-day hard drive for our computers, where we are aware of what we store, we add more files to it on a daily basis and are able to retrieve any files when needed. Alternatively, implicit memories are our unconscious memory, consisting of feelings, images and sensations. This is extremely important because when a traumatic event occurs, not only is the memory impacted in processing the event, but it is affected long after the event has passed and is linked to post traumatic stress responses (PTSD) (Van der kolk, 1994; Mcnally, 2005). In practical terms, when a traumatic event takes place, explicit factual/long-term memory is compromised, however, implicit memories remain intact, storing the feeling, images and sensations of the experience. Thus, when individuals with traumatic pasts develop PTSD and experience a common symptom, flashbacks or reexperiencing the trauma, this is the implicit memory coming into play, compelling the person to experience the images, feelings and sensations in real time (Mcnally, 2005). This can occur in children who have experienced trauma as well, which is why avoidance of trauma reminders is a coping tool used here to avoid this unpleasant reexperiencing. Bessel Van Der Kolk in 'The Body Keeps the Score' focuses on body memories and their importance in understanding dissociated trauma (Mcnally, 2005). Basically, research has shown us that trauma physically alters the body and our stress responses (i.e., fight, flight, freeze, and fawn) for human survival. It puts us in overdrive, in survival mode, as seen in PTSD survivors experiencing hypervigilance, altering the way they even relate to everyday experiences. Imagine for a second, how disturbing and distressing it is to hear someone yelling somewhere from where you stand, something that we may hear or experience often, even on the street, and this reminds you of a time when you were being yelled at and physically hurt extremely badly. Our minds act as if it is reality right now, not distinguishing that this was in the past and our body believes whatever our mind tells it, reacting to it in real time. Hayes (2015) reaffirms in his research that trauma memories are the physiological imprints of past experiences, which dictates the way a person thinks, feels, or copes with the events in life following this.

In understanding this, you may be able to now also see why researchers have spent years exploring traumatic memory loss to factual events that take place, often called Traumatic Dissociative Amnesia (Van der kolk 1994, Mcnally, 2005). Experts argue that this forgetting on part of our explicit memory system is a way our mind protects itself from the most horrific lived events (Mcnally, 2005). As several theorists point out, our memory follows certain functions, as the rest of the faculties of the human body, however, trauma disrupts functions, playing by entirely different rules. Due to trauma and memory being an infamous topic among several fields with numerous perspectives, McNally (2005) points out that there are also a lot of myths about it out there. So, let's debunk some of them to avoid any confusion. (1) Memories of trauma are rarely truly lost, they live in us in several ways, including being repressed into our unconscious minds or as discussed, in our bodies; (2) memory may seem photographic, but they are not played by a video recorder, despite how the media may make it seem, we cannot always press play and see it like a movie (Mcnally, 2005). When a person recalls any experience from his/her past, they reconstruct the elements of the memory, piece by piece using several parts of the brain (Mcnally, 2005). However, due to this, we must make an interesting point, it is likely that individuals who have experienced trauma several years ago or during childhood may not be able to recall the traumatic event chronologically or with complete accuracy, as memory can fade over time or aspects of the events are repressed or detached from. It can be equally likely that, for some individuals with complex severe trauma, aspects of a traumatic event from years ago or childhood can be recalled well, in the way it was stored. Let us also note, recollection of implicit memories can be made several years following a traumatic event, due to the nature of storing this type of memory, as mentioned previously. Finally, Mcnally (2005) mentions that (3) not thinking about a traumatic experience for a period of time, does not mean that the individual is unable to recall it, this is detachment or an avoidant coping mechanism.

Similarly, we also have looked into research of early childhood experiences of sexual abuse in adult victims, that state that early traumatic experiences in these adults is dependent on information from a child's perspective (i.e., the age the traumatic experience took place). Now, it is common knowledge that young children's memory may not allow for concrete narratives, understanding/logical/moral reasoning, intelligence, and full storage capacity during the time the event occurred, obviously based on their age too (Becker, 2014; Barry et al., 2018). Also, let's not forget that the length of abuse or trauma and level of severity are factors that impact the intensity and availability of traumatic memories (Goodman et al., 2019). Regardless, working with children and/or adults of childhood abuse involves recollecting events either in terms of body sensations, vivid images and feelings (explicit memories) or in terms of narrative and a conscious timeline, and reframing, processing and rewriting the narrative in a way that is healing to the survivor/victim. We use survivor or victim both here and later since some individuals who have experienced trauma refer to themselves as survivors as this is empowering and uplifting revealing their resilience, strength and a way that allows them to rewrite the narrative of this experience. However, others refer to themselves as victims and detest being called survivors as it devalues the pain and hurt they have been through. In keeping the term victim for themselves, they acknowledge that it was not their choice or in their control to be hurt, abused and mistreated. This allows them to validate their painful experience and have others emotionally attuned to their pain with empathy as well. Both are valid and for this reason, we choose to write both of them here.

Finally, it is important to mention a common consequence of trauma that results from mental health conditions and coping responses, that is addiction or substance abuse. Research shows us that early childhood trauma alters a child's very malleable brain in adapting and developing under stressful circumstances. What this means is that certain neurotransmitters that should function in a particular way, due to trauma, reorganize the brain, altering it to now function differently. Recto and Lesser (2021) mention that an amount of four traumatic experiences in childhood could result in adult alcoholism later in later life; as self-sedation is usually a beginning for individuals to numb themselves. Although, we will also point out, that even one early childhood traumatic experience or Adverse Childhood Experience (ACE's) and other forms of distress can also lead to addiction and does have links to anxiety, depression and PTSD as a way of self-medication to cope (Recto and Lesser, 2021). But, what really happens here is that through these traumatic experiences, children begin to form unconscious beliefs about themselves or others or the world, some may include that: they are not lovable, they are defective, they are not important, they are not worthy and so much more. These beliefs will then drive their behavior later in life into relationships that may make them feel similarly and retraumatize them. Often, to cope with this, self-numbing is a viable option which can be chosen. When we are children, we numb ourselves by dissociating, detaching from the experience emotionally or through a medium like television or games. As adults, we have a variety of ways to detach from pain, often, pain we have repeatedly experienced for decades. Addiction is a much more complex subject as well, because as we mentioned above, trauma reorganizes neurotransmitters in our brain to adapt, this means we might be lacking in some neurotransmitters as a result. For example, the neurotransmitter that provides us the feeling of pleasure, dopamine, or the neurotransmitter that provides us feelings of happiness or love, these are serotonin and oxytocin. We should have an abundant amount of these as children, as they are naturally produced in our brains and connected to how our parents hold us, show us safety, warmth and love as infants and young children. But, if our parents do not provide us with what our brain and body needs, we will begin to lack these and then as adults, when we find a drug like marijuana or heroin or cocaine that begin to produce these neurotransmitters in excess and give us what we were lacking; love, happiness, pleasure, euphoria, we may then become hooked onto them. We will not explore this in more detail as this is a subject to be explored on its own entirely, requiring a book of its own. But, it is vital to understand that addiction is the outcome of pain, trauma and abuse. It is often not something wrong with the individual, but what happened to them.

By now it seems evident that trauma affects us in a variety of ways. But, it does not only involve childhood abuse, rather, when looking into cultural elements of trauma, studies discuss how immigration and asylum-seeking processes produce a plethora of traumatic experiences for individuals. It is important to mention how war, famine, political uprising, financial inequalities/poverty, loss of a home or country, natural disasters, social inequality (i.e., racism, sexism, ageism, oppression, prejudice, discrimination), societal persecution/abuse, and escaping such environments are at present, major causes of trauma and related mental as well as physical illnesses. Saadi et al. (2021) mentions that asylum seekers in the US have an extraordinary challenge, to convince the government that their necessity for shelter is valid, as they are too fearful to return back to their home country. This group of individuals are exposed to extreme traumatic stressors, revealed through psychiatric symptoms based on past torture and current mistreatment (Saadi et al., 2021). The results are seen through deficits in cognitive functioning (e.g., memory lapses, short term memory loss, head trauma) and mental health difficulties such as prolonged severe depression or PTSD. According to Saadi et al. (2021), in a study with a group of 200 asylum-seekers, 69% were getting diagnosed with PTSD and 55% with depression. Physical head trauma was found to be a factor in 30%, while 68% reported that they were subjected to physical abuse and 20% were suicidal. The study also revealed that memory loss was seen in 21% of 40 asylum-seekers. However, we want to also note again that, immigration and migration are traumatizing stressors in itself as repeated adaptation and acculturation to a new world can cause a lost sense of self. Simply put, not only is the journey to get to another safe country where we may not be harmed distressing, but figuring out who we are when we get there, losing the person we once were and trying to fit into a new world can be emotionally and mentally taxing, without even factoring in any violence observed or the loss of loved ones when trying to flee. Culture is a huge element when discussing any topic, especially trauma, as each cultural worldview, beliefs, coping mechanisms, expression patterns and behaviors are unique. In order to fully understand and help individuals, it is valuable to recognize the role their cultural background plays as well. We will be discussing this in the next chapter. Similarly, it is also worthy to mention the impact of trauma related to medical illnesses, injury, postpartum difficulties following birth of a child, loss of an organ etc. Responses to such events are similar to any traumatic or abusive event as mentioned previously and have effects on cognitive, emotional and behavioral levels too. Such experiences change an individual's belief about themselves, the world and others, leading to mental health difficulties for years.

Chapter 2

Culture

Before delving any further, it is important to clarify that cultures can in a broad sense be categorized as individualistic or collectivistic. Individualistic cultures refer to systems in which, each individual governs for themselves and their own unique thoughts, feelings, self-sufficiency and independence rather than focusing on the needs of a larger group such as the family, community or society (Engelbrecht and Jobson, 2016; Sharma, 2021). Individualistic cultures include regions in the west such as Europe, the United States, the United Kingdom, Australia etc. Whereas, collectivistic cultures mean individuals comply with social norms, attune one's self to groups (i.e., family, community, society, the culture as a whole, their thoughts, feelings, beliefs and practices) and group perspectives. This culture often highlights traditional ideals, obligations to others (perhaps hierarchies), maintaining relational or group harmony, following rituals with specific group beliefs and perspectives to maintain the group as a whole (Engelbrecht and Jobson, 2016; Sharma, 2021). Collectivistic cultures include regions such as Asia, Africa, the Middle East as well as, Latinx cultures and parts of Eastern Europe too (i.e., Greece).

Research also shows us that cultural beliefs impact a person's subjective meaning of trauma experiences as well as their process of accepting traumatic memories, either in a helpful or unhelpful manners to cope with and heal from such an aversive event (Engelbrecht and Jobson, 2016; Schnyder et al., 2016). More simply, culture basically provides the context on how an individual understands experiences, the world, themselves and others. It also determines how one might think, feel and behave based on cultural norms, beliefs and perspectives. For instance, in individualistic cultures, evaluations of the self being exposed, vulnerable or insufficient were mutual, however, collectivistic cultures are centered more on evaluations by others and how this may affect social functionality (Schnyder et al., 2016). Individual outcomes following trauma like PTSD have shown cultural variations. A common example of how culture affects trauma can be seen in certain group-based cultures, where individuals who have suffered rape are unable to share this due to fear of bringing shame onto their families, causing the individual more torment and suffering overall, as discussed in video testimonies of trauma survivors (Schnyder et al., 2016). We feel it is important to mention that, in some of these cultures, rape outside of marriage can also lead to honor killings (i.e., killing the individual who has suffered the rape) in order to preserve the family's identity in society and avoid shame. This, in itself, is a traumatic thought let alone following a horrific event. This is common in Arab/Middle Eastern cultures as well as Asian cultures. Since this exploration includes a majority of participants from the Middle East, we mainly emphasize collectivistic cultures. However, some of our participants also come from Greece, which is considered a mix of collectivistic and individualistic worldviews according to our studies. Greece shares similar group-based beliefs as most collectivistic cultures while maintaining a spot in an individualistic region of Europe which has its own unique influences on the country/population as well.

By now, thinking of collectivistic cultures, the value that is placed on group solidarity and balance is evident. Due to this, sacrificing one's personal needs, goals, or struggles to maintain the group harmony is quite common (Singh-Manoux and Finkenauer, 2001). This can be sacrificing oneself to provide for one's family (e.g., financially, practically), taking care of others more than oneself, ignoring/tolerating maltreatment or wrongful behavior, silencing oneself and so on. Oftentimes, this can involve a lack of sharing of experiences or painful highly charged emotions to close support systems due to shame. As Singh-Manoux and Finkenauer (2001) reveal to us, sharing is more common with friends than family members in such cultures (which we can link to family hierarchies and other beliefs). If you can think of situations or experiences where you have experienced the above or know of others that have, can you link it to beliefs stored relating to some cultural views? Connecting this to trauma, it is common that silence or avoidance is used as a coping mechanism in collectivistic cultures due to fear, shame, lack of understanding and several other reasons. Moreover, emotional expressions, especially in public, in certain collectivistic cultures are considered immature and one's own difficulty in controlling themselves (Wing Sue & Sue, 2013). A control of emotions or lack of it at times is seen as strength here too. Tending to the physical needs of others (e.g., cooking, cleaning) shows care and love in these cultures, especially among women (Wing Sue & Sue, 2013). In group cultures, fathers are said to be highly authoritarian and distant, while mothers are more responsive but less emotionally nurturing, often serving as a mediator between father and child. It is not uncommon for both parents to use verbal or physical punishments as a form of learning (Wing Sue & Sue, 2013).

Members of collectivistic cultures are more disposed to depression when experiencing a negative situation and are less likely to seek out support during stressful times to avoid burdening others. This leaves them isolated, alone, and helpless, bringing about additional mental health concerns (Sharma, 2021). Something important to point out in such hierarchy-based cultures is that gender inequalities are not uncommon, mainly inequalities related to women being inferior and the need for them to be more submissive, polite, obedient, self-sacrificing etc. This may make it more likely for mental health struggles to rise and leave women more prone to trauma and abuse. In the long run, it is likely for children in these cultures to grow up quite distant from emotional experiences and thus, face difficulty coping with difficult emotions in the future or manage past trauma. It is important to keep these cultural elements in mind when reading some of the stories in order to have a more comprehensive understanding of perspectives and worldviews that are unconsciously in the background of each story.

Chapter 3

Our Exploration

We wanted to take a closer look into the experiences of parenting and trauma, its consequences both struggles and successes of individuals from two cultures to gain understanding of different yet similar worldviews. Trauma was implicitly explored through the interviews to link back to our literature. This insight is especially important as there is a lack of ethnographic, narrative information from Kuwait as well as Greece, that explores such topics from this angle. Our aim is to provide a subjective insightful look into several life experiences, get a better understanding of child rearing practices with a culturally informed perspective, generational effects as well as negative and positive outcomes.

All of that being said, what we really wanted was to hear you, relate to you, allow you to share your story and express your choices. Mainly to help others relate to this and feel like they aren't alone, everyone is in the same boat and we are all trying to figure things out. So, when reading these stories, we invite you to really allow yourself to open up emotionally and connect to each person, think about how you can relate this information to your life and what you might take away from their experiences.

THE PROCESS

We will provide a variety of logistics below to demonstrate an overview of how and from whom stories were gathered. One of the investigators who conducted the interviews is a Kuwaiti national and shares a unique insight into the Kuwaiti culture and how it applies to the experience of expats living in Kuwait. The other investigator has studied, lives as well as works in Greece and has extensive professional and personal experience living within the Greek Mediterranean culture. The final investigator was not part of the interviews and did not participate in any of the data gathering process. In order to prevent bias in the interpretation of data received, different investigators were involved in distinct processes to maintain a structured set of ethical boundaries. We conducted semi-structured interviews with participants residing in Kuwait and Greece, from a variety of mixed nationalities. There are a total of twenty participants, consisting of both parents and their children (in some stories), ages ranging from 10 to over 65 years old and of both genders. Both married and divorced parents participated. They all come from several life stages; from school students to working individuals to retirees.

All participants were contacted via phone or instant messaging to inquire their interest in participating in the current ethnographic study regarding life successes that made them well-rounded individuals, influenced their parenting styles and coping methods or consequences. After they agreed and verbally consented to participate, a time for the interview process was set. The interviews were conducted through online platforms such as Zoom to comply with COVID-19 regulations and to ensure everyone's safety. The interviews were audio-recorded for transcription purposes, only to ensure accuracy in interpreting and presenting their stories in our research. They were informed of this and that all information shared would be kept confidential with their participation being voluntary as well as anonymous. To ensure their anonymity and privacy is maintained, we use pseudo-names (i.e. made up names) for each participant and no original names are mentioned. They were asked a series of questions during the interview to help guide their narratives and gain necessary information. Questions differed for a parent or a child, however, they were linked, paralleled and reflected one another. Interviews lasted from 30 minutes to 1 hour.

Questions were formulated to incorporate several stages of life to gain a better understanding of past experiences, upbringings, career choices, any consequences and effects on parents and children. Parental questions explored elements of how the parents' past and early life experiences have translated to their own parenting styles and its impact on their children. The following questions were asked to all parent participants; (a) What was your inspiration behind your parenting approach? (b) What was helpful and what did you avoid? (c) Give us background information on yourself growing up and learning about different things, (d) What should you not do or should avoid while raising children, and how was it different from your upbringing? (e) How did you keep your children motivated? (f) What values did you instill in your children? (g) Share some successful stories about being a parent.

The questions given to the rest of the individuals (the children of the parents) were constructed to mirror similar questions asked to their respective parents, serving as a parallel reflection revealing outcomes. We wanted to observe the effects or outcomes of the parenting techniques that most of the parents chose to employ and examine how successful they were for their children. The following were the questions; (a) Describe yourself in five words and explain why you chose those five? (b) What motivates you and how did you stay motivated growing up? (c) Share a memory from your childhood that shaped who you are today, (d) There's a lot of research that talks about positive relations between parents and children, what do you think parents of successful children have in common? (e) Which lessons are you going to pass down onto your future children, and would you do anything different?

The information and stories gathered from the interviewees help provide a personal and subjective understanding of how trauma affects individuals in a variety of ways and how that may be translated generationally as well. We attempted to look into how parents raise successful healthy ideal individuals and if there was a specific pattern found or was each case different.

Chapter 4

Stories From Greece

Before proceeding with the following culturally based narratives, it is vital to emphasize that the interviewer and researcher of this particular section is seen as an expert immersed in Greek culture for a substantial amount of years. The participants from Greece were chosen based on voluntary participation in sharing their subjective perspectives of parenting and childhood.

STORY 1: PATRICIA

Patricia begins the interview by sharing that she is in her 50's and has two children, her son is 25 and her daughter 15 years old. Her son is an engineer and her daughter is still currently in school. She has a lengthy academic background, with a bachelor's degree as well as a master's degree in History. She also obtained higher education in Organizational Psychology and a PhD in Social Sciences. She currently works as a trainer and career counselor at a University. After getting some initial demographic information from her, she was asked the interview question 'what was the inspiration behind your parenting approach?' Here, Patricia discusses that throughout her children's upbringing, she was quite active in gaining additional education while working full time simultaneously. She mentions how, often, this is the cost of balancing education, work life and having a family, for women. This can be connected to societal gender norms, where women are habituated from a young age to be empathetic, social, nurturing caretakers who are responsible for maintaining a family's well-being. Whereas, men are socialized towards physical, practical, competitive, problem-solving activities involving accomplishments (financial or otherwise) making them the socially viewed 'BreadWinners' (Lyons, Brewer and Bethel, 2017; Sharma, 2021). When a woman takes on both roles of a nurturer and a worker, challenging societal gender norms, often the consequence is having less time to fully care for a child as intended. Due to this, she delegated much of the parenting to her parents, especially with her son's upbringing and less so with her daughter. Linking this to Bornstein (2012) who pointed out that culturally based rearing is focused around the demands, needs and survival of the group. Moreover, in collectivistic cultures like Greece, there is an in-group bond and obligation towards others, therefore, a child is often raised by the entire system, family and community to maintain relational accord (Engelbrecht and Jobson, 2016; De Greck et al., 2012). Patricia's choices are understandable when accounting for cultural influences that follow group perspectives, to ensure the survival and functionality of each group member and the well-being of the whole system (Engelbrecht and Jobson, 2016). Several works mention that in collectivistic cultures, high importance is placed on group balance, in order to maintain such harmony, it is common that members of the group share in sacrificing personal needs and attuning themselves to care for others who are in need, especially when it comes to child rearing, to preserve the systems equilibrium (De Greck et al. 2012; Singh-Manoux & Finkenauer 2001). Moreover, tending to the physical needs of others such as cooking, cleaning and nurturing is a sign of attention and affection in such cultures as well (Sue & Sue, 2013). Patricia felt that, sometimes, her parenting style could be viewed as distant, however, this was mainly due to the fact that she was juggling quite a lot and needed the help. As Patricia stated this, her anxiety of having to cope with so many responsibilities can be felt from afar, even in thought itself. It is typical to feel empathetic towards working mothers as this is a common and draining reality for many women in the 21st century. The psychological toll of having to take on various life roles apart from being a nurturer can result in having less energy, mental reserve and emotional capacity for a child at times.

She goes on to discuss her childhood and relationship to her parents origin. Her father was a ship captain, which meant he traveled often and was not home for long periods of time. This left her mother responsible to raise her and her siblings. It is important to note here that these gender roles reflect traditional cultural norms of men sacrificing themselves to provide for their families and being distant, while women care and nurture the family (Sue & Sue, 2013; Lyons, Brewer and Bethel, 2017). Cuddy et al. (2015) described this as men stereotypically being independent and goal oriented, while women are viewed as interdependent as well as oriented to others. Since, men are socialized to more physical activities and strain than women, it seems evident why traditionally when Patricia was growing up in the 70's, more traditional gender roles were followed by her parents (Lyons, Brewer and Bethel, 2017). Additionally, she recalls how it was overwhelming for her mother to handle parenting on her own. Patricia remembers going on holiday with her aunt instead of her parents and her grandparents living with her to help out. She emphasizes that in Greek culture, it is quite common that the family as a whole raises the children, similar to the literature. She explained that if one member cannot take care of the children, someone else from either the immediate or extended family would come to help. This is how her childhood was and likewise, this is how it was when she was raising her children too. Greek culture, similar to any other group-based culture, such as Arab, African and several Asian cultures, also incorporate the extended family in rearing practices, it is a familiar concept. This is a wonderful view of social support; to be able to divide the responsibility when needed and this also allows a child to experience different perspectives, learn various family roles, build knowledge and adaptability. As Chen (2012) suggested, a child's relationship to larger family systems, apart from parents, builds social wellness and resilience, especially during instances of distress. Moreover, Masten and Monn (2015) point out that resilience has been studied over decades, both at the level of each child and the family as a system. The family has been proclaimed as a key component of the research on risk and resilience as both an adaptive system and a setting for human development. Resilience is generally described as "a dynamic system's ability to successfully adjust to changes that jeopardize its functionality, survivability, or development" (Masten and Monn, 2015). Resilience is also the ability to successfully adapt in the face of adversity, which is often deduced from evidence of successful adaptation in the wake of major obstacles or systemic disruptions. When adjustment to a significant disruption is taking place, it is easiest to see resilience "in action." However, resilience can also be inferred from data showing that the system (i.e., family) is "likely" to respond effectively given the assets and adaptive capabilities at its disposal. Building system capacity for constructive responses to disturbances is frequently the aim of efforts to prepare people, families, communities, and other systems for impending challenges (Masten and Monn, 2015). The paradigm of family resilience changed focus from the family as a source or protective structure for the individual family members to the functions of the family system as a whole, examined in terms of family adaptability or maladaptability in the face of adversity, as well as the family processes that promote familial resilience (Masten and Monn, 2015). Erik Erickson (1963, 1968) also suggests the division of labor and shared household responsibility is an important stage of psychosocial development and growth for an adult. With this in mind, one could assume that the entire family unit working together to help Patricia take care of her children while maintaining a work life balance is a part of familial adaptation and resilience to adversity, it may also include cultural elements and psychosocial growth, or all of the above. However, one may wonder how conflicts between extended family members and parents raising the child may arise, differences in discipline, morals, perspectives and communication, which might also be confusing for a child.

Patricia describes choosing a different way to raise her children compared to how her parents raised her. When she was a child in the 70's, almost 50 years ago, she recalls the mentality being different and parents being stricter. It is important to note that cultures that employ authoritarian parenting, as will be evident soon, do so in an attempt to uphold order in the system to function appropriately (Bornstein and Bornstein, 2007; Smetana, 2017). Her home life was quite systematic, she was not allowed to go out with friends, go to sleepovers or go on holiday even at the age of 16 or 17. This was a revealing statement to the type of parenting that was employed during the 1970's. As mentioned previously, parenting practices can follow either a supportive position or a controlling one, with responsiveness and demandingness governing the two polarities (Baumrind, 2005; Kuppens and Ceulemans, 2019). Baumrind's (1971) typology defines authoritarian parenting as a way of forcefully governing, influencing and evaluating the child's behavior based on strict rules. Similarly, controlling parenting involves psychological and behavioral governing of a child's life. Patricia describes her parents using behavioral control through restricting her from being social or independent, implementing rules, demands, disciplinary schemes and monitoring rewards (Kuppens and Ceulemans, 2019). Erik Erickson's theory of Psychosocial Development comes in well here, as it states that if a child lacks the opportunity to explore stages of psychosocial development—in this case, the dichotomous stages could be considered stage four: industry versus inferiority in preadolescence and stage five: identity versus confusion during adolescent years. As a result, a secure sense of self may not be formed, or optimal development associated with exploration and engagement with the outside world autonomously may be lacking, leading to increased anxiety, negative worldviews about themselves, others and the world, and identity struggles in adulthood (Erikson, 1963, 1968; Pittman et al., 2011). Moreover, Patricia describes additional aversive experiences, like corporal punishment was still common in schools at the time as well, where teachers preferred to use sticks to punish or discipline children, similarly, at home it was not uncommon to receive physical punishment to discipline children. She implies that her home life involved such physical punishment since it was the norm at the time, which was difficult, and she did not like it. Physical punishment is again, an excessive form of the behavioral control type of parenting that is viewed as trauma inducing for a growing child and is linked to negative outcomes such as PTSD, depression, anxiety, suicidality and behavioral issues (Cohen & Mannarino, 2008; Jaberghaderi et al., 2004; Kuppens and Ceulemans, 2019). With the combination of physical control and discipline not only at home but in schools, one can view Patricia's experiences of several forms of physical abuse as traumatic and even as an adverse childhood experience (Cohen & Mannarino, 2008; Jaberghaderi et al. 2004). Howe and

Fearnley (1999) also discuss how physical abuse by parental figures is linked to insecure attachments as the parent is the source of fear and distress to the child, leading to the child living in survival mode, emotional dysregulation, vulnerability, loneliness and anger (Sharma, 2021). As we know from Karen Horney's research, children need safety and security from attachment figures for personality development and forming a secure sense of self in adulthood. Coupled with the lack of independence Patricia received, deep attachment and mental health struggles are not uncommon.

When trauma is involved, it is likely for children to develop oppositional behaviors, as suggested by Cohen & Mannarino (2008), the traumatic experience during childhood felt as unfair, unjust and wrong. Patricia displays the advanced outcome of such an upbringing by stating that she has raised her children differently from her own parents as she promotes freedom and autonomy with boundaries. She describes allowing her daughter to go out with her friends, knowing who she is with at all times nevertheless, but still permitting her independence as well. Patricia's moderation of appropriate control reflects Kuppens and Ceulemans' (2019) argument that specific amounts of parental control can lead to a positive effect on childhood development by promoting learning, structure, stability and routines. Patricia does not use physical punishment at all with any of her children and this was an important distinction for her compared to her parents. She truthfully revealed how hurt and sad she felt experiencing physical punishment which is something that she still remembers with disdain 50 years later. This heartfelt statement can be linked back to the emotional weight physical abuse leaves and the trauma that is stored as a consequence, that drives each parenting decision and approach. In very simple terms, she did not want her kids to feel such sadness or pain as she did from adults who were supposed to protect her. It is a common emotion anyone can relate to when they have experienced such punishment, the sadness is consuming, especially for young children who cannot cope nor understand such intense emotions and upheaval in their inner system. Additionally, Ainsworth (1979), Bowlby (1969) and Sutton (2019) state that due to the unpredictable and unreliable nature of parental figures as safe and secure providers, attachment insecurity may develop when controlling parenting is practiced. The attachment relationship with the parent becomes the source of alarm and distress causing the child to be overwhelmed with feelings of helplessness, hopelessness, vulnerability, loneliness and abandonment (Finzi et al., 2001; Howe and Fearnley, 1999). In return, this feeling of vulnerability is flooded by pain, anger, distress, dysregulation and feeling out of control. Two of the most extensively studied risk factors for the onset of insecure attachment are maltreatment and family violence (Sutton, 2019). Consequently, children perceive their parents as unsupportive, unresponsive, dismissive, and aggressive. Children who had experienced abuse had an 80%

higher likelihood of having an insecure attachment style than children who had not, according to a new meta-analysis examining young children (Sutton, 2019). Importantly, current evidence demonstrates that childhood maltreatment, including emotional, verbal, sexual, and physical abuse, is all related to the development of an insecure (either anxious or avoidant attachment style) during childhood and adulthood (Sutton, 2019).

However, Patricia kept certain values from her upbringing, replicating them with her children and these include: being honest and not lying to the children, being a role model, calmness, no arguments or conflicts or mess at home, politeness, integrity and ethical behavior towards others. She also makes sure to show her children the value of money as she wants them to understand that money requires effort, so that they do not overspend. Patricia feels that her parenting style is realistic and a well-balanced one with boundaries as well as affection, therefore, children can learn what is acceptable and what is not, but still feel supported enough to make mistakes and learn from them. Patricia takes on a authoritative parenting approach (i.e., high in demand and responsiveness) with reasonable expectations of the child, effective communication, warmth and attunement is seen (Baumrind, 1971), reflecting the supportive parenting practice as mentioned by Kuppens and Ceulemans (2019). She is responsive, involved, and validates her children and promotes altruistic behaviors towards others around them. This form of parenting has very positive developmental outcomes including preventing behavioral difficulties, substance use and declining mental health issues (Baumrind, 1971; Kuppens and Ceulemans, 2019). From her experience as a career counselor, she points out that she feels distant parenting at times can be better than overwhelming controlling parenting. She has noticed that with Greek parents, who over-love, over-protect and over-worry for their children; they are always preparing to have things ready for their children. When she gets a student in her office for career counseling, most times, she can tell what sort of parents they have and the parenting style that was used. In her opinion, this does not give children the life skills that they will need as adults. This is another form of parental control through psychological means. As discussed in research, this form of intrusive influence of a child's inner and outer world can be traumatic as well, as a child's loss of developmental stages linked to autonomy, identity, industry, initiative, authenticity and personality development is affected (Erickson and Erickson, 1998; Schultz & Schultz, p. 163; Tian et al., 2019). Since, we have mentioned how this ties in with Erik Erickson and Karen Horney's theories in the introduction chapters, it may seem evident now how psychological parental control also leads to several negative outcomes including depression, inferiority, struggles with self-esteem, anxiety, aggression and deviancy during childhood and later on in life (Pittman et al., 2011; Kuppens and Ceulemans, 2019; Tian et al., 2019).

It is important to note that Patricia observing that Greek parents often employ controlling forms of parenting, either psychological or behavioral, culturally is understandable as such forms of parenting maintain group homeostasis and similar values. Yet, it is also an interesting insight into how deep traumatic and emotional regulation goes in such cultures. Parenting to Patricia needs to be cool, calm, with perspective and balance. She mentions that for her, "parenting is raising adults, not raising children." This puts a lot of the parenting literature we looked into in the first few chapters into perspective. Her statement really is one to reflect on; parenting is a process of raising well-adjusted adults and as she mentions, too much of something is never helpful and has negative aftereffects.

To the question "how did you keep your children motivated?" Patricia responds by stating that she is not sure if you can motivate children to do something they are not personally interested or invested in. A valid point, as this would be projecting your own interests onto the child rather than allowing them the space and encouragement to focus on what they are truly interested in, which is far more beneficial. She mentions that her son did not do well in his exams to get into a university, however, he managed to get into engineering school and currently works for a large Greek airline as an engineer, following his own path. Her daughter already knows she would like to pursue psychology as her first degree to become a clinical investigator. She has even researched it, made preparations about potential universities and seems confident with that path. Patricia fully supports the paths her children chose and thinks that perhaps, since her children continuously observe her studying, doing seminars and working hard, this serves as a motivator. She mentions how she openly engages and involves her children in these aspects of her life as well, she takes them to her seminars, workshops, book presentations, graduations or college events as well. Further evidence of Patricia's use of authoritative as well as supportive parenting is the aspect of modeling or demonstrating as an adult, adequate behavior, control, emotional regulation and how to handle obstacles (Baumrind, 1967, 1971, 2005; Kuppens and Ceulemans, 2019). Modeling goes back to how children learn about the world through the social learning theory; if parents model specific behaviors including hard work and prosocial attitudes, children tend to mimic such mannerisms and learn through observation (Sharma, 2021). In this case, perhaps Patricia's modeling of commitment, curiosity, determination and social involvement serve as motivating factors and learning opportunities that her children have internally stored. She states that parents cannot really motivate children because it depends on the child, their personality and thoughts that they have. Patricia openly absorbs herself with her children, welcoming discussions about life and the future, as well as, supporting her children in any decision. She always tries to give her children plenty of opportunities to try new things and see what is out there in the world, she encourages them to explore and be exposed to all options. Looking at Patricia's parenting approach through the attachment perspective, we can see how she has formed a secure attachment with her children, providing them with protection, care, security and support to be who they are (Howe and Fearnley, 1999). Due to this, identity, social and personality development follow a positive trajectory as well. She says, perhaps if her open communication with her children is not a sole motivator, exposing them to her life and other opportunities can be an additional motivator. Listening to Patricia speak about herself being a role model and always seeking out opportunities for her children to be exposed to life's many joys brings about feelings of empowerment, motivation, encouragement and opens room to the possibility of continuous growth.

Finally, Patricia shares that during the COVID-19 lockdown, when she was at home full time, she really enjoyed spending time with and taking care of her children. She realized during this time how much her children needed her and attuned to them. She mentioned that she would not want to go back to a life of working 12 hours a day and being away from home. Even though, when she worked in person, she still spent time with them, but it was always time split in half and she felt like she may have missed some things. Whereas now, since she got to experience being home with them continuously, she has realized the difference. She says that the whole lockdown period has changed her as a parent and as a person. Patricia also recently completed a degree, training in Mental Health and Counseling and she discussed how by studying that, she learned more about herself, her behaviors and reactions, similar to Ellis's ABC model we discussed previously (Opre & Opre, 2010). It has also helped her understand her children and her family as well. Towards the end of her interview, a warm-hearted atmosphere was felt as she emphasized that despite her children being at an age where they are merging into adulthood, she continues to be fully invested in them. Her sincere story of how the COVID-19 pandemic has helped her connect with her children more, sheds light on small subjective positive effects of an entirely negative period in many individuals' lives. Despite the world being at a standstill, some were still moving internally, growing, making connections and evolving for the better.

Unfortunately, Patricia's daughter was not available to participate in the interview.

STORY 2: SARAH & NICK

Sarah is 49 years old and has two sons, ages 19 and 17. Her son Nick was interviewed shortly after her and his account is presented later on. She was asked the first question, 'what was the inspiration behind how you decided to parent your children?' to which she boldly responded, "to do the opposite of what my mother did to me." She explained how she did not like the way she was raised as it was not nurturing or caring. She felt that in her family of origin, as a child, nobody cared about her and she felt as though she did not even exist. She had no rights, no voice to express her needs and she felt invisible. This is the heart-breaking truth, she shares, that was so painful and she did not want her children to feel what she felt. A first glimpse into Sarah's interview, we already begin to observe which parenting method may have been employed by her parents. As we discussed previously, this could look like parenting is quite rigid, with caregivers managing and implementing demands and rules onto a child as a form of discipline either psychologically or physically (Kuppens and Ceulemans, 2019). However, in Baumrind's typology (Martin, 1983; Baumrind, 2005), this form of parenting can be seen as neglectful with low demand and low responsiveness by the parental figure, which mirrors Sarah's sentiment as well. One can also suggest that this is a form of emotional neglect which are actions or inactions by the caregiver that may result in the child developing behavioral, affective, or mental disorders (Hildyard and Wolfe, 2002). Children who have experienced parental neglect often display difficulties in self-regulation as well as control and civic responsibility, low autonomy, antisocial traits, depression, anxiety, psychosomatic complaints and poor academic performance well into adulthood (Kuppens and Ceulemans, 2019). Sarah's experience reveals childhood emotional neglect and trauma, that is, caregivers being unresponsive to the child entirely, unable to attend to the child's distress, emotional and/or social needs and as with controlling parenting, expect children to regulate difficult experiences alone (Teicher and Samson, 2016). Moreover, through an attachment lens, neglectful children are more likely to have anxious or avoidant (i.e., insecure) attachments to their caregivers and later in life (Hildyard and Wolfe, 2002). Likewise, Perry (2002) notes that childhood neglect or inadequate attention to needs does not allow for a secure attachment relationship to be formed between caregiver and child. As mentioned earlier, attachment is a child's first bond with another person, the very first relationship in life that allows for the formation of beliefs of oneself, others and the world. As Perry (2002) suggests, when there is a lack of secure attachment, the child is unable to feel safety, comfort, pleasure, or regulate intense distress with the help of the caregiver's warmth. Similar to Karen Horney's research suggesting that safety and security is vital in attachment formation and development (Schultz & Schultz, p. 139). Without this, the child's nervous system (fight or flight) is unable to be soothed during stress and that might make them highly sensitive to stress throughout life. The child essentially learns that they are unloved, rejected or unworthy, others are not reliable, the world is lonely or dangerous and these beliefs get programmed into the child. These core beliefs come out later in life as difficulty in socio-emotional navigation, emotional regulation, behavioral issues and allows them to be predisposed to other mental illnesses, more so when combined with controlling parenting reinforcing such beliefs (Perry, 2002). This was evidently displayed in Ainsworth, Blehar, Waters and Wall's (2015) 'Strange Situation' study, where children whose attachment figures ignored their needs or had a delay in responsiveness or responded in an egregiously insensitive manner, learned that the caregiver is unavailable or unresponsive. Therefore, the child similar to young Sarah, may be more anxious and apprehensive of her parents as she is uncertain on what to expect, this lack of stability in the attachment figures behavior is said to lead to an insecure anxious attachment (Ainsworth, 1979). Teicher and Samson (2016) point out that children who experience childhood maltreatment and trauma are more likely to experience depression, substance use, anxiety, eating disorders, suicidality, psychosis and personality disorders as a result. Similarly, alcohol, anxiety, depression, and drug use issues are also more likely to occur in people with an insecure attachment style (Sutton, 2019). Several forms of childhood maltreatment play a role in such a prevalence, these include childhood physical abuse, sexual abuse, emotional abuse and neglect as well (Teicher and Samson, 2016). Several detailed analyses suggest that different forms of childhood abuse or adverse early childhood experience are associated with alterations in brain functionality and structure, especially in cases of childhood neglect (Felitti et al., 1998; Avdibegović and Brkić, 2020; Teicher & Samson, 2016; Perry, 2002).

When Sarah became a mother, she wanted to be a good one who was loving, caring and nurturing, she wanted the mother she did not have, she says. As Cohen & Mannarino (2008) demonstrate, some children who have adverse childhood experiences respond to the injustice with oppositional tendencies and this seems to include parenting distinctly opposite to what they had experienced to avoid transferring similar pain and trauma onto the next generation. Similarly, with Sarah, she wanted to offer her children the best through a supportive parenting stance, but at the same time, did not want to spoil them. She mentions how she never favored any of her sons, as her parents did with her. Her parents always told her that she was their favorite, but often treated her like a servant, compared to her sister who received all the attention. She was so deeply hurt and could not fathom how her mother could favor or separate her and her sibling the way she did and this possibly led to a difficult relationship with her sister. Linking this to Zervas and Sherman (1994) who suggest that perceived parental favoritism is an important element in the development of identity, beliefs or perceptions of oneself and others later in life, affecting general self-esteem. Fairness, the opposite of favoritism, is a western norm that refers to consistency and appropriateness in meeting one's needs (Bedford, 1992). Considering Sarah was raised in Greece, a collectivistic world in the 1970's, it is possible to assume that fairness may not have been a focal point in cultural views nor cultural parenting practices. Politically, Greece was ruled under a dictatorship until 1974, where the concept of fairness may not have been a reality for the nation. Moreover, in family systems, it is found that non-favored children express feelings of anger, depression, rejection, unworthiness and inferiority towards their sibling with overall well-being decreased, whereas favored children experience positive (e.g., more safety, acceptance, superiority and adoration) and negative consequences (e.g., sibling jealousy, distant sibling relationships, self-centered, guilt and lager expectations from parents) (Zervas and Sherman, 1994). Similar to Sarah's statement, theories of equity and social comparison postulate that parental favoritism lowers the quality of sibling relationships, increases conflicts, hostility towards other siblings and the lack of closeness in adulthood (Suitor et al., 2009). It is seen that recollections of maternal favoritism during childhood puts a strain on sibling relationships as siblings such as Sarah are unable to ignore their mother's favoring behavior and this later reinforces insecure attachment, negative views of oneself and core beliefs of being unloved as discussed previously (Suitor et al., 2009). Bedford (1992) also finds that parental unfairness and favoritism leads to less affection and increased conflict in parent-child relationships, including with adult children. Sarah's continued confusion and sadness by her mother's actions can be seen as a consequence of favoritism, neglect and controlling parenting, affecting her and their relationship till this day. It is important to emphasize that childhood memories of unfairness or maltreatment continue to affect the parent child bonds throughout life and these are also the long-term effects of trauma; we see this evidently with Sarah who is still trying to decipher her mother's behavior (Bedford, 1992). If we look at this through the ABC lens mentioned earlier by Albert Ellis, the activating event (A) is Sarah navigating parenting her own two children, the beliefs (B) resurface from her own childhood reference of parenting reminding her she was not cared for, treated unjustly, rejected, hurt and not loved, leading to her consequence or emotional outcome (C), continued feelings of confusion, anger, sadness, and oppositional behaviors with her own children as to not recreate intergenerational traumatic pain (Opre & Opre, 2010).

Sarah describes herself as quite a strict mother, who also shows her children love, that they are a priority and mean the world to her. She feels that she has succeeded in that. She is very emotionally supportive and was genuinely concerned about her children's needs and wants. It is a two-way relationship for her, she asks them questions and seeks feedback. She wants to know what they want, what satisfies them and what works. Sarah accurately demonstrates applying Baumrind's authoritative parenting (1967, 1971, 2005) with high demandingness and high responsiveness as well. Similarly, this form of supportive parenting approach incorporates her parental involvement, emotional acknowledgement and responsiveness to her children's needs through feedback and the re-assessment of her methods. Through this approach, she also models to her children how to cope with distress and conflict through communication, compassion and empathy which is another aspect of supportive parenting. However, she always sets clear boundaries and maintains consistency (Baumrind, 1971; Kuppens and Ceulemans, 2019). As we have seen through literature, a certain structure and parental control through repeated routines is important for learning and development, which in this case, control can be seen in a positive light (Kuppens and Ceulemans, 2019). On the other hand, she shares how sustaining such constancy was difficult, as she was the only one maintaining such behavior since her husband traveled frequently and upon his return, he lacked the same steady boundaries, limits and uniformity. This meant that the children were often confused by certain parental fluctuation, however, as she took a more prominent role in the parenting dyad, it helped the children feel safe, secure and satisfied, as they have openly shared with her. Referring back to Bowlby (1969) and Ainsworth's (1979) theories on attachment, Sarah's warm responsiveness to her children's needs, involvement, attunement, close proximity, consistency and stability provides a secure base for her children to develop secure attachments. This is based on the child viewing Sarah as an accessible, reliable and trustworthy attachment figure. Due to this, she noticed that when her children began growing up, they did not prefer being in environments with other children who lacked boundaries or limits, as they felt it was chaotic. In our exploration of beliefs or as Bowlby (1969) refers to it as "internal working models," one of the beliefs or worldviews we learn from our home and caregiving environment is how others and the world works or looks like. Since Sarah's children have been adapted to calmness, self-control, stability within nourishing limits, this can explain why viewing the opposite of this in other circumstances can be overwhelming.

She continues by stating that she has always fostered open communication with her children regardless of topic. She discussed their feelings and supported them, making them feel safe/comfortable. She made sure her children had a voice to express their curiosities, concerns, opinions or thoughts from a young age and she would always explain herself when she set boundaries, as well as apologize, admitting when she was wrong. She mentions encouraging her sons to finish anything they started, it may have seemed stern at the time, but as she asks her children about it now, they tell her that she was right to do so and appreciate it. Considering Erik Erickson's theory (1963, 1968), Sarah fostered a space and atmosphere to explore the different stages of social identity development appropriately, accomplishing favorable outcomes with trust (stage 1), autonomy (stage 2), initiative (stage 3), industry (stage 4) which refers to competently learning, understanding mastering skills and secure identity formation (stage 5) (Erikson, 1963, 1968; Erickson and Erickson, 1998). Additionally, Sarah modeling prosocial behaviors of taking responsibility for her mistakes and apologizing emphasizes modeling through the social learning theory and in that, her children learned through her example to accept mistakes, put themselves in others shoes and compassionately problem-solve, an important component of emotional as well as social intelligence (Sharma, 2021). Distinct to how her parents raised her, where she felt non-existent with no ability to speak up for herself, she gave her children a voice to share what they wanted but maintained a voice for herself as well, making it a balanced and equal environment. She feels that she has learned a lot from her children, one of which includes learning how to raise sons, as she was raised with sisters and was worried she wouldn't be able to navigate the gender differences, but through them, she learned a lot about the nature of men as well. Sarah's insights emphasize the difference and importance of not only parenting but fostering a secure parent-child relationship. Russell, Mize and Bissaker (2002) explain that parenting emphasizes only the caregiver and specific practices, or approaches used in rearing such authoritarian, controlling, permissive, supportive etc., but, a relationship is a series of interactions across a period of time between two individuals who know each other based on beliefs, values, characteristics and the environment. Thus, a parent-child relationship accounts for both the parent (thoughts, reactions, feelings, behavior) and the child responses (thoughts, opinions, feelings, reactions, behaviors) (Russell, Mize and Bissaker, 2002).

Sarah mentions that she may not have been the best mother when her sons were very young, as she was working quite a lot. But before delving into obstacles and impacts of working mothers, it is important to mention that according to the findings of Yusuf and Sim (2017), working mothers often employ an authoritative parenting style (i.e., supportive parenting with firm limits, as seen with Sarah) which has a favorable significant association with child-parent relationships, appropriate control, and overall contentment. Authoritative parents, such as Sarah, are more effective at teaching children appropriate social behavior, which they can absorb and call on in later interactions with their peers. Furthermore, authoritative parenting has a beneficial association with regulating spousal relationships as well (Yusuf and Sim, 2017). Children with authoritative maternal parenting have higher self-acceptance, supervision, adolescent school achievement, psychological autonomy and positive developmental outcomes which we will observe in our following interview with Sarah's son Nick.

Continuing on, Sarah wishes she could have spent more time with her sons, but after work, the moment she got home, she threw off her heels and rushed to the ground to engage with her sons. She recalls how difficult it was raising her first son, because she was working full time and this was in the early 2000's when her company was not quite accepting or supportive of her being a working mother. She was the only woman in her department, as well as being the youngest with a lot of responsibility. Sabat et al. (2016) discusses the challenges faced by women in the workforce balancing motherhood along with additional unjust gender differences and discrimination. There are four theoretical models that explain the distinct components of discrimination experienced by working mothers which include: the Stereotype Content Model, Role Congruity Theory, Social Role Theory and Stigma Theory. Sabat et al. (2016) state that mothers experience significant stigmatization as this identity is perceived negatively in workplace settings and are subjected to negative stereotypes and prejudices leading to judgment and lack of sympathy. According to the Stereotype Content Model, stereotypes can be classified into two categories: warmth and competence (Sabat et al., 2016). When working women become mothers, they run the risk of being stereotyped as either homemakers (who are seen as warm but lacking in ability) or female professionals (who are viewed as lacking warmth but highly competent). Research shows that mothers in the workforce are often rated as less dedicated, incompetent, impromptu, hired less and recommended lower salaries, compared to non-mothers (Sabat et al., 2016). Based on these stigmatizing stereotypes of mothers, to be a mother in the workforce may imply high levels of stress with dual responsibilities of shutting off a part of one's nurturing identity to be seen as professional when on the job and turning it back on once at home, putting the body in continued state of alertness to comply to each environment. This continuous split of one's identity on a daily basis can take a toll on one's mental health, belief of oneself and the world being unaccepting or rejecting important parts of them and inevitably leading to depression, burnout, anxiety and even, health difficulties (Sabat et al., 2016; Yusuf & Sim, 2017). Apart from stereotypes, social and cultural roles contribute to the differential treatment of women in the workforce, as women are often perceived to perform domestic roles, especially in collectivistic countries such as Greece, whereas men take on industrial and financially beneficial positions earning them titles of "breadwinners." These roles infer double standards in the workforce when it comes to family, as women with children are deterred or intentionally outworked from high-status positions, while men with children are boosted and urged into high positions to provide for their family and are evaluated more positively and research has found this is evidence of the "fatherhood bonus" (Sabat et al., 2016).

Sarah's feelings of not being a good mother during her work period can be linked to the Role Congruity Theory that suggests following stereotypes of "ideal workers" is in direct conflict with perceptions of what it takes to be a "good mother." Individuals assume that a "good mother" is constantly present for her children, whereas the "ideal worker" (i.e., the most capable worker) prioritizes the job over all other obligations. This distinction gives the impression that these two principles are mutually exclusive or that one cannot flourish in both roles at the same time (Sabat et al., 2016; Yusuf & Sim, 2017). As Yusuf & Sim (2017) postulate, working mothers begin experiencing feelings of guilt when they are not able to provide full attention to their children and their loss of quality time, as seen with Sarah. Furthermore, it is assumed that as a woman becomes a mother, she would become less engaged in her work. Sarah mentions how men at work would smoke around her despite her telling them she was pregnant, as well as, male co-workers giving her extra work, knowing she was pregnant. She kept trying very hard to be productive and push through, but this inevitably impacted her. Especially when she was pregnant, she cried daily and was continuously suffering from stress and anxiety. Stigmatization of mothers occurs not just when others learn that a female employee has children, but it also affects female employees who are about to become mothers. According to empirical studies, pregnant employees face a variety of negative consequences, including discrimination, negative stereotyping, social rejection, lack of sensitivity, job role testing, demotion and economic disadvantage (Sabat et al., 2016). As a result, disclosing one's pregnancy status or other pregnancy-related information may expose pregnant employees to more prejudice, which current meta-analytic research shows is both medically and psychologically harmful. Undeniably, qualitative data reveals that pregnant employees minimize or hide pregnancy-related information in their professional relationships, particularly from their superiors, in fear of losing control in the position, if the pregnancy is made public (Sabat et al., 2016). These findings point to the need for authenticity over discrimination avoidance and is evidence of the impact faced by pregnancy discrimination in the workforce not only on psychological and physical health but towards social and professional trajectories. Balancing both family and work in itself is a source of stress, burden, cultural pressure and systemic trauma to an entire gender of individuals without even including aspects of parenting or other life stressors. Rajgariah et al. (2021) reveal that working mothers and subsequently their children suffer from more stress (68% greater) and depression than non-working mothers, with age and education, not revealing a statistically significant predictor of stress effects. However, the physical, mental, and financial pressures of caring for two or more children of similar ages might result in health-related stress, as seen in Sarah with two children without a large age gap (Rajgariah et al., 2021). According to alternative research, parents who have family support have reduced parental stress, yet in Sarah's case, she mentions a lack of support as well as a lack of spousal support (Rajgariah et al., 2021). Due to these high demands and the maintenance of multiple roles, it undeniably has implications on her overall wellbeing (Yusuf & Sim., 2017).

Sarah learned only 3 years ago that her stress affected her pregnancy as she was exposing her baby to her high levels of cortisol. Lautarescu, Craig and Glover (2020) suggest that the prenatal environment in the womb has sensitive periods, especially during brain formation. It is explained that prenatal stress increases maternal cortisol that becomes neurotoxic to the brain development of the fetus, although immune functionality also influences prenatal and postnatal development as well (Laplante, Brunet and King, 2016). Sarah's awareness of cortisol effects on child development and temperament is evidenced by research that reveals that Prenatal Maternal Stress (PNMS) subsequently impacts children with growth (physical and cognitive), nutrition, bonding, temperament, poorer linguistic, attentional, emotional regulatory, behavioral and intellectual consequences as well as low birth weight and mental wellbeing (Laplante, Brunet and King, 2016; Oyetunji and Chandra, 2020). Temperament, according to Laplante, Brunet and King (2016) represents behavioral characteristics that are consistent across age and contexts and are assumed to predict later psychological performance. Mothers who have experienced adverse life events during pregnancy, or who have higher levels of pregnancy-specific anxiety or depression, report that their children have more difficult temperaments (Laplante, Brunet and King, 2016). Werner et al. (2007) state that children of mothers experiencing Prenatal Maternal Stress show increased heart rate when stressed as well as greater motor and crying reactivity rates. This finding suggests three working theories by Werner et al. (2007): infant crying behavior and mother's emotion dysregulation are displays of similar genetic emotional dispositions characterized by lengthy and prolonged reactivity; mood-based differences in mother's physiology (i.e., anxiety, depression, stress) can influence the early developmental determinants of crying reactivity; women who experienced prenatal mental illness, or stress maintained this mood dysregulation postpartum, which had a negative impact on their emotional availability and parenting, and, as a result, their child's early self-regulation skills (Werner et al., 2007). Sarah describes experiencing this post pregnancy, when her son was born, regardless of how much she tried, he kept crying and screaming all the time (i.e., temperament/emotional reactivity and dysregulation). She learned that she had created an anxious, neurotic, overly stressed baby that couldn't sleep or be soothed easily. There is evidence of a link between maternal depression, anxiety and stress and nocturnal awakenings in children as well (Oyetunji and Chandra, 2020). Early sleep disorders (short sleep duration and nocturnal awakenings) have been linked to emotional and behavioral issues during childhood development and can be linked to nervous system dysregulation mentioned above (Oyetunji and Chandra, 2020). Her son Nick did not want to be held, or touched which resulted in her exhaustion and becoming agitated too, representing temperament changes and reactivity discussed above. This then became a vicious cycle because the baby would react to her frustration of trying to hold him and feed him with anxiety and it would make her more restless/frustrated. The vicious cycle Sarah speaks of is discussed in Werner et al. (2007), where their research postulating that maternal mood dysregulation postpartum is maintained and perhaps, worsened which negatively affects the child's regulation skills becoming more reactive and worsening her mental state, almost going round into a loop while juggling external stressors as well. As Sarah shares these vulnerable, painful and guilt-ridden parts of balancing work, her pregnancy and an anxious child, she begins crying. About 2 decades later, this part of her life is still so painful.

Post-partum, she faced several other difficulties like going to the hospital frequently because she was over lactating or not lactating enough and had to painfully struggle to throw bottles of milk away daily. She had a rib fracture from the pregnancy, lightheadedness, gastric reflux issues, continuous fevers and suffered from a case of insomnia. She cries while saying that for the first 2 years of her son Nick's life, he was behaviorally reactive, screaming all day long, wouldn't sleep even though she tried everything; even changing 4 doctors, all sorts of alternative methods and nothing helped. These postpartum years of her first son's birth made her feel like she was not a good mother and she has been asking her son for forgiveness ever since she found out how she had played a role in affecting him. Our children form attachments with us and feed off of us, therefore, if we are stressed, they are stressed and they express it through screaming and crying since for a baby, that is their language. Sarah describes the impact and struggle in coping with traumatic childbirth experiences and postpartum stress. Beck and Watson (2008) described birth trauma as an incidence that occurs during any stage of the childbearing process and involves the mother or infant suffering real or threatened serious damage or death. An unfavorable consequence, such as postpartum bleeding, fracturing, breaking or tearing of body parts or psychological discomfort might be classed as trauma (Beck and Watson, 2008). A woman's response to this extraordinarily traumatic stressor can be through profound levels of anxiety, helplessness, increased stress, loss of control and fear. Beck and Watson (2008) suggest that stressful labor and delivery (i.e., Sarah fracturing a rib and facing health struggles), emergency cesarean birth, and psychosocial stress or discomfort is associated with childbirth trauma and a delay in lactogenesis (the process of producing abundant milk causing breastfeeding difficulties). Past research additionally suggests that maternal mental health difficulties may be associated with not enough food supply when the baby is hungry or inability to suck breast milk properly which also plays a role in development (Oyetunji and Chandra, 2020). This theory supports a strong link between maternal mental health, insufficient nutrition in childhood and weight/growth limitations. Breastfeeding has been reported to play an essential role in the mental health of new mothers as well because of its ability to down regulate the HPA axis circadian rhythm and reduce stress responses by activating the nervous system, according to some research (Oyetunji and Chandra, 2020). Moreover, postpartum anxiety (PSA) has a similar deleterious influence on infant nutrition and nursing. PSA is caused by stress and a hormonal imbalance, specifically a reduction in Oxytocin and Prolactin levels, which inhibits the milk ejection reflex and subsequently, appropriate breast milk production. In its function in the evolution of maternal behavior, oxytocin (often known as the "love or cuddle hormone") stands out among other hormones such as progesterone and prolactin in the emergence, manifestation, and maintenance of maternal bonding and caregiving behaviors (Oyetunji and Chandra, 2020). Thus, the inability to adequately breast feed, as Sarah describes, not only hinders production issues of oxytocin that is necessary for bonding, soothing, experiencing love and attachment with the child, but consequently, increases stress both for mother and child, again leading to a vicious cycle of helplessness and further exacerbating post-partum stress and trauma.

For her second child, Sarah was stressed with juggling work, her first child and her second pregnancy as well, which led to a doctor recommending she take a sick leave from work for 3 months. She was at home for the last trimester of her second pregnancy, which led to her second son being less anxious and calmer after birth. She feels that she had not slept the 5 years her sons were born while juggling work and home life alone since her husband was traveling for work frequently. As a result, from her increased stress levels, she quit her job which was a hard decision she chose to make as she had an incredible career for a woman at the time, leading a high-profile European project. She then moved to Germany for a few years due to her husband's work and felt it was the right choice; she wanted to be a better mother and worked hard to create a relationship with both her sons during this time.

To the question 'how did you keep your children motivated?,' she responds by stating that she empowered her children to feel confident. Her mother had done the opposite with her, leaving her feeling disempowered and unmotivated, therefore, Sarah did not want that for her children. She helped her sons believe in themselves as she believed in them. Her sons also tell her that observing her handle so many obstacles and continuously showing up for them made her a role model and someone to look up to. As discussed earlier, this coincides with the Social Learning Theory of modeling appropriate behavior and regulating oneself despite the challenge, which once more demonstrates her use of supportive parenting again (Kuppens and Ceulemans, 2019). She also mentions encouraging them to maintain the value of commitment, especially when they were young, she made sure they finished anything they started and always explained to them why. For example, her sons used to take Taekwondo classes and she insisted they finish classes rather than quit since it was important for their survival. She says that they appreciate it now and have even continued participating in other forms of martial arts. But, she also fosters an open humorous environment where they feel comfortable to communicate with her on all sorts of topics, including intimate ones which can be motivating in itself, as it diminishes any fear they may have had discussing uncomfortable subjects. Additional values she encouraged with her children included: integrity, honesty, family, consistency, purpose and need for joy. She explains that studying psychology later in life, in her mid-40's, has helped her understand herself, her children, others and change her entire worldview. Her going back to school in the middle of her life allowed her children to observe her through this challenging phase which also served as a motivator, demonstrating that it is never too late to follow your passions.

Some success stories Sarah mentions include how her sons talk about her to peers, emphasizing that they are proud of her and all her accomplishments. She feels that they are inspired and that's what makes her successful. Interestingly enough, one of her sons is also considering a career path in the field of psychology, modeling after her recent journey. Throughout Sarah's story, it is evident that as readers, we were also taken on a journey, from childhood emotional trauma to gender discrimination, system and work struggles to pregnancy trauma and anguish. All this trauma however resulted in a deep and profound connection forming between her and her children and led to her success as a mother, as an individual and as a worker. Her story is inspiring in not only showing your kids firmness and love in equilibrium, but also revealing that parental mistakes and flaws can be overcome with effort, despite biology, leading to positive parent-child relationships and healthy fully developed adult children.

Nick, who is Sarah's oldest, began his interview by describing himself as "intelligent, lazy at times, curious, interesting, moody and an overthinker." Nick says what keeps him motivated is having limits and goals, for instance, having deadlines and structure from a professor. But, if he likes a task or activity, he is eager to do it right away. However, if he is not interested in it, he may engage in procrastination at times. He also mentions how teachers or professors who are strict, in a manner that pushes him to work harder, help motivate him as he appreciates such firmness. He mentioned that home life was quite structured with certain rules and it really helped him become organized, prepared and calm. We can evidently observe how Sarah's authoritative and supportive parenting influences have played a major role on Nick's personality and preferences, how he relates to others and the world.

To the question "share a memory from your childhood that shaped who you are today," Nick responded by describing two years where he and his family lived in Germany between 2005–2008. He was 4 years old when they arrived in Germany and when they returned back to Greece, he was 6 and a half. He discusses having a noteworthy kindergarten experience in Germany, where he felt encouraged to be different, to think outside the box and take part in creative activities that involved making things with his hands. It motivated him to learn and be curious about several subjects even at the age of 4, he mentions he knew how a car worked, what the gas was used for, how the handles internally functioned, etc. Due to his curiosity to find out how things work, his family expected him to pick a career in engineering, however, he is currently in university pursuing agricultural studies since he was also very interested and curious about science. Children with authoritative parents such as Sarah are innately motivated, curious, and interested in learning, like to solve their own problems, and choose tough projects, according to research (Baumrind, 1967, 1996, 2005; Kotaman, 2013). These children, similar to Nick, are also seen to have a high sense of self-worth, making it simpler for them to choose difficult tasks or fields as well (Kotaman, 2013). Nick is at the top of his class in university now and shows similar ambition to Sarah. We might also assume here that Sarah's open communication with her children and her allowing Nick to be curious about things, ask questions, express his opinions, at home and elsewhere, has also played some role in making him an inquisitive, smart and dedicated young man.

Nick believes parents who over-spoil or overindulge their children may not have successful children. He thinks, perhaps having successful parents to serve as role models is vital for children to strive and to be like them, but he also believes that perhaps, children with parents who may be struggling to maintain day-to-day needs may motivate children to work harder to have a better life than their parents did. He shares that he really admires his mother and that her career is spectacular for a woman in Greece. He claims that she used to travel to several countries for work and was extremely dedicated in trying to provide for him and his brother. Even though she was not home often, he says it was useful watching her go to work, expressing ambition made her an invincible idol of success. This coincides with what Sarah described as her view of being a successful parent, being an authentic inspiration to her children. What he found useful during his upbringing was that his mother tried to make him and his brother independent from a really young age in several ways, for one, he knows how to cook, do the dishes, iron, clean and care for himself. He will definitely pass down lessons and values of independence, responsibility, life skills (e.g., cleaning, cooking), good manners and continuously striving for more (e.g., more knowledge) to his own children. This is how Nick described being successful internally as a person; balancing external success to career paths and assets earned. He learned these from his parents and wants his children to believe in this as well. However, he shares that at times, his parents were overprotective (e.g., telling him to stay away from children who had bad behavior) and strict with technology (e.g., not having a PlayStation, or Nintendo to prevent harm to their eyes). He wouldn't implement such misconceptions or strict limits when raising his children because he feels they are not rational beliefs and do not work well in rising children in an upcoming technological world. His last point about technology and overprotection are perhaps also linked to the differences in generational understanding of such subjects 40 years ago, when raised in the 1970's, individuals were not adapted or familiar with technology and could explain Sarah's approach of avoiding technology use at home. However, currently it is 2023, technology is increasingly embedded into everyday life and serves positive purposes as well. It seems understandable that future parents like Nick will be more open to integrating technology as a part of parenting practices.

STORY 3: GEORGIA & PENNY

Georgia, a mother of 4 children, begins her interview discussing the inspiration behind her parenting approach. She states she wanted her children to be able to be free, to explore and have the opportunity to be creative. Additionally, she wanted them to feel that it was acceptable to think outside the box, be comfortable enough to have unique thoughts and feel differently. Creativity was one of her main motivations. In some ways, this paralleled her own upbringing as she had very few limitations since her parents were not very strict and had few expectations of her and her siblings, providing them with freedom. She aimed at creating a similar atmosphere with her children. Her parents mainly wanted her to have a college education and to be independent, especially because they were 6 girls from an immigrant Italian family in the 1970's in the United States. Her father did not want his children to feel that they had to get married to survive. He wanted them to have an education as this was the way he felt freedom was achieved. However, despite education being very important to her parents, they never imposed on her or her siblings what to study, or a career path they had to take, making them free to choose their own paths. Georgia's parents employed a version of supportive parenting that incorporated warmth, empathy and acknowledgement of individuality that benefits emotional and cognitive development, well-being, achievement and learning resourcefulness (Kotaman, 2013; Kuppens and Ceulemans, 2019), however, they also incorporated Baumrind's (1967, 2005) permissive parenting style as well, as permissive parents are slightly more tender, offering increase in autonomy rather than control. Permissive parenting involves high responsiveness yet low levels of parental control or guidance

(Baumrind, 1967, 1971, 2005). Parents that are indulgent do not force their ideals, norms, or regulations on their children. They go over the house rules and explain them, avoid using harsh, punitive, or traditional disciplinary methods and have little authority and make few demands (Baumrind, 1967, 1971, 2005; Kotaman, 2013). They do not aid their children during decision-making processes or certain chores that involve responsibility, in order to foster their freedom (Baumrind, 1967, 1971, 2005; Kotaman, 2013). Parents do not intervene and guide their children's decisions, actions, and behaviors until they ask for it. Indulgent parents are a resource that their children can tap into whenever they choose. Children have many rights, and parents, on the other hand, endeavor to meet every demand and need the children have (Kotaman, 2013). Permissive indulgent parents see their children's independence as allowing them to pursue whatever interests them; the parent's responsibility is to safeguard and care for the child, similar to Georgia's father permitting her to choose a career path on her own. They attempt to raise independent individuals who can establish their own life by respecting the child's originality (Baumrind, 1967, 1971, 2005; Kotaman, 2013). Although, it should be noted that despite this form of parenting taking place, opportunity for secure attachment is still present due to the warm emotional responsiveness of the caregiver, boosting the child's sense of security in the attachment relationship by allowing the child to form an internal working model of the caregiver as being accessible, dependable, and trustworthy. The child is more open to stimuli that may spark exploration of the external (others, the world), as well as the interior dimensions (the self), based on the caregiver's stable attachment, safety, and presence (Ainsworth, 1979). On the other hand, Kotaman (2013) also suggests that this form of parenting does not allow for children to face and overcome challenges through the support and appropriate modeling from parents on how to problem-solve, regulate distress and cope with adversity. Similarly, Erik Erickson (1963, 1968) emphasizes parental guidance is a requirement while children go through imperative stages of psychosocial development resolving conflicts, aiding children during these formative stages promotes self-regulation and psychosocial growth (Erickson and Erickson, 1998; Pittman et al., 2011). Studies on permissive/indulgent parenting reveal associations with both internal (such as anxiety, depression, detached behavior, psychosomatic symptoms) and external outcomes (such as academic misconduct, delinquency, problematic coping), as well as with interpersonal skills, self-esteem, problem solving abilities (Kuppens and Ceulemans, 2019). Although, as countless studies reveal, permissive indulgent parenting can have harmful effects on child development by allowing freedom without responsibility for children who developmentally are not mature enough or ready to manage such full independence without guidance, this is also context dependent (Kotaman, 2013). When viewing permissive parenting in Georgia's narrative, it is vital to understand this approach in terms of immigrant parents; the research shows an association between altering cultural parenting practices to the new system and the host culture (Nesteruk and Marks, 2011). Corroborated by Erickson's attention to cultural and historical contexts in which meaningful associations of each psychosocial stage are uniquely derived (Erickson, 1963,1968).

Nesteruk and Marks (2011) suggest that immigrant families' habits change as they acculturate and their parenting practices shift as well. Many factors influence the impact of changes on the family system, including family structure, ethnic background, culture, immigration motives, socioeconomic level, and English proficiency. Immigrant children are seen to acculturate and become Americanized faster than their parents (Nesteruk and Marks, 2011). Literature shows that immigrant parents from many countries have reported being less authoritarian, lenient, and more involved in their children's lives after being exposed to the now child-centered host culture. Our own observations of employing permissive parenting during immigration suggests, parents themselves are learning to adapt to having less control in the host culture and need to remain lenient to ensure their survival and freedom in the new world as a minority. Therefore, as these novel associations transfer over into the parenting realm, it is then as a domino effect, projected onto the children as well. These parents establish more open communication with their children as they spend more time in the western culture, adopt new techniques like reasoning and negotiation and give their children more power, especially if they have come from a less liberal or authoritarian culture, as seen by the data (Nesteruk and Marks, 2011). As a result of the host culture's influence, as well as the lack of social support from extended families that many immigrant families were accustomed to in their home countries, fathers become more actively involved in their children's lives as well. Similar to Kotaman (2013) postulations, it is found that as immigrant parents grow more permissive, their children's self-esteem rises and their rates of behavioral problems rise (Nesteruk and Marks, 2011). Immigrant parents, however, fully support their children acquiring education and cultural competency to succeed in the host society; as observed in Georgia's recollection of her father promoting her to seek out a college education (Nesteruk and Marks, 2011). Nesteruk and Marks (2011) found that immigrant individuals perceive assertiveness and social communication skills as a factor in building confidence and future success for their lives in American society. In their view, having such skills as well as education would ensure the survival of the group. Thus, when considering Georgia's father's main rule for her and her sisters to be educated and acquire knowledge-based skills, this comes from a collectivistic view of safeguarding the endurance and survival of the immediate system and his daughters that are embedded in it.

Societally, Georgia explains how she also grew up in a time where the US had a lot of riots and anarchy which can be viewed as traumatic witnessing as well. Her family was always empathetic, bringing in African American children into their homes which was unheard of in "white" neighborhoods. Her parents actively sought to integrate them with other cultures and races. Prosocial or altruistic behavior is described as the deliberate act of assisting others, irrespective of the goal. It is a multifaceted phenomenon involving individual behaviors based on thoughts, beliefs and feelings, and explains the manner in which individuals are aligned towards others during solidarity acts (i.e., helping, volunteering and sharing) (Marti-Vilar, Serrano-Pastor and Sala, 2019). It is related to emotional and social intelligence, as well as culture. Marti-Vilar, Serrano-Pastor and Sala (2019) found that higher helping and empathic prosocial behaviors were positively correlated with collectivism and individuals from collectivistic worlds. Interdependence and social (e.g., family) obligations are valued in collectivistic cultures to maintain societal and group harmony (Wong, Konishi and Kong, 2021). Since Georgia's parents are from Italy, which similar to Greece can be seen as a blend of individualistic and largely, collectivistic mindsets, it is important to emphasize cultural influences on social behaviors. According to the Social Learning Theory, this includes parents modeling to children appropriate social attitudes when interacting with others and learning empathic behaviors (Wong, Konishi and Kong, 2021). Wong, Konishi and Kong (2021) propose that prosocial tendencies start early in life and increase throughout adolescence. Previous studies have shown that parents play a significant influence in the development of prosocial behaviors in their children. Different theoretical ideas infer the link between parenting and prosocial tendencies (Wong, Konishi and Kong, 2021). One source of indirect evidence is the attachment literature, claiming that children who are securely attached to their parents are more likely to be prosocial, as a sense of security is established when parents are not only responsive and sensitive, but also supportive of their children's explorations, thus, authoritative and permissive parenting are more likely to foster prosocial development, as evident with Georgia (Ainsworth, 1979; Baumrind, 1996, 2005; Wong, Konishi and Kong, 2021). Furthermore, because children form an internal working model of themselves, the world and others based on their experiences with parents, children with sensitive and responsive parents may be more likely to offer aid to others, as a result of the representation that others are deserving of equity, care and that their needs should be met through helping (Wong, Konishi and Kong, 2021).

When Georgia moved to Greece at an older age, she was bothered by how Greeks back in the early 1990's were racist to the immigrants coming in. Greece was and still continues to be a hub for immigration, along with facing economic difficulties and a refugee crisis, began growing discriminatory attitudes across time (Lefkaditou, 2017). Georgia did not want her children to be raised with such a worldview, due to her upbringing in the U.S with her parents being culturally diverse, open-minded and modeling acceptance, it was helpful in her conveying and teaching similar values to her children residing in Greek culture. One of Georgia's degrees is in Political Science and she still considers herself a political activist. She gets involved in issues of inequality and injustice and her children display such behavior as well, especially speaking up when injustice is observed. A clear association can be observed through the lens of the Social Learning Model as to how Georgia developed prosocial behaviors from her childhood and intergeneration-ally projected these attitudes onto her children, making it a focal point of her career (Wong, Konishi and Kong, 2021). It is important to emphasize the insight Georgia provides as to the similarities and differences in 1970 America compared to 21st century Europe, as well as generation differences of life in a globalized world. Although a lot has changed for the world since 1970, a lot has also stayed the same in that racism is still largely prevalent and not always discussed commonly in collectivistic societies. She feels that, often, her parents were too open and flexible, which did not give her much guidance at some point, similar to previous research suggesting a lack of guidance seen in permissive parenting can lead to consequences (Baumrind, 1967, 1996, 2005; Kotaman, 2013). Parents, according to Kotaman (2013), should be involved in their children's learning process and act as scaffold-ers. Literature shows that parental involvement in their children's social and emotional development has a positive impact, not through solving problems for them (which takes away their learning opportunity), but by giving them the means to tackle difficulties appropriately (Baumrind, 1967, 1996, 2005; Kotaman, 2013). Due to her parent's open permissive nature, she explains that she lacked direction in college, as she had two majors in her under-graduate degree and has never had a real job (which she appreciates about her life path as well). However, with her own children, Georgia provided more guidance on where they wanted to go in the future while still emphasiz-ing a sense of freedom and support for any choices they sought. Georgia's parenting demonstrates a supportive authoritative approach in which parents are loving, affectionate, caring and responsive. These traits are also indica-tive of psychological well-being. These parents recognize their children as unique human beings who have their own distinct character and personality (Baumrind, 1967, 1971, 2005). On the other hand, distinct to permissive par-ents who choose to acknowledge their children as fully evolved and mature people; authoritative parents do not hold such perspectives nor employ puni-tive, harsh disciplinary tactics to guide their children; instead, they use mod-eling, reasoning, justifying, explaining, and monitoring as seen in previous interviews as well. Authoritative parents have more securely bonded children, who are more school ready, higher achievers, have less mental health issues, and are happier in life, according to research (Kuppens and Ceulemans, 2019; Kotaman, 2013).

Georgia shares that her parents had a very strong sense of ethics and a firm value system (e.g., to be good people) which is also observed in how she chose to raise her own children. She also emphasized other values which include being true to themselves, following their hearts, not complying and following the crowd, accepting being different, honesty to themselves and others. She herself is very honest with her own children about everything as she feels it helps them be more comfortable at home. Honesty can be considered an element of supportive parenting as it not only models ethical behavior but is a tool in explaining and reasoning rules or demands to children, aiding in logical thinking and problem-solving development (Kotaman, 2013; Kuppens and Ceulemans, 2019). It is, of course, a clear demonstration of authoritative parenting as well as discussing extensively the importance of clear effective communication, with honesty playing a large role (Baumrind, 1971). On the other hand, she worries that perhaps too much honesty may make children feel as though everyone is over involved with each other's lives and creates difficulty in maintaining one's own privacy. She feels that this is a tricky consequence of too much open communication and dialogue, but she is accepting and happy when her children tell her something private to them. To her, this demonstrates her children's ability to assertively instill certain boundaries they need, including with her. As authoritative parents support children within limits and boundaries, it seems highly likely that children learn such behavior and employ them when necessary in their lives and relationships (Baumrind, 1971; Kotaman, 2013). Thus, revealing the positive impact of such parenting coming full circle as children display it right back to parents in the future. Georgia tries to continuously be mindful that her children need their privacy and tries to stray away from the traditional Greek/Italian cultural enmeshment of the family as a group. She is content knowing that there is balance between her children feeling comfortable to talk to her about anything while at their own discretion.

Georgia continues to maintain a parental role without blurring the lines too extremely into a friendly role with open communication as her children become emerging adults. She realizes differences in generations that play a role as well, she explains that the biggest difference she finds with her generation and her children, is the electronic age which has emerged. When her children were young and developing, she restricted mobile phone usage until they were 18 years old. She felt that it was not necessary until a certain age, for example, with her oldest receiving a phone in 9th grade. They were permitted computer usage for limited hours and for educational purposes. She felt electronics would hinder their creativity and imagination when it came to non-academic purposes, instead, she encouraged them to play outside, social-ize with friends or be inventive instead. Today's technology pervades every aspect of a child's life in increasingly accessible forms with multipurpose and interactive capabilities (Vittrup et al., 2016). Crayons, paper, and clippers, for example, are unanimously regarded as beneficial instruments for children's growth, however, electronic devices such as television, mobile phones, MP3 players, video games, and computers, have sparked increasing debate about their developmental appropriateness, with some studies recommending them for young children while others wary of the potential harmful consequences (Vittrup et al., 2016). Literature has revealed that using technology and media for educational purposes has been connected to improving mathematics skills, vocabulary usage, prosocial behaviors, vocabulary, and school preparedness. In addition to increasing spatial skills, visual attention, problem-solving, fine motor coordination, computer literacy, and academic achievement, video games are also beneficial to children. Computer use has also been linked to greater cognitive exam scores and success in science-related subjects (Vittrup et al., 2016). However, cognitive limits prevent young children from compre-hending the purpose and application of these technologies in the same way that adults, or even older children and adolescents, do. Children with these cognitive limitations are unable to critically assess the complex uses and meanings of various media technologies, leaving them susceptible to negative influences such as violent content, unsuitable pictures and messages, persua-sion and inaccurate representations of reality (Vittrup et al., 2016). Therefore, it is unknown if technology use stunts creativity, as Georgia perceives, on the contrary, research shows that within limits and meditation, technology usage can be useful for building skills and creative minds. However, it is vital that parents and caregivers participate in and oversee their children's media con-sumption to ensure a balance of usage is maintained, as Georgia discusses and that is another example of authoritative supportive parenting. Parental media mediation, as Georgia demonstrates, refers to conversations between parents and their children concerning media use (Coyne et al., 2017). When parents impose restrictions on the content or time spent watching media, this is known as restrictive mediation. Parent-child media dialogues, as well as parental initiatives to teach children critical viewing abilities are referred to as active mediation (Coyne et al., 2017). Although the effects are moderate, research on parental mediation has indicated that some forms can be good for children's cognitive and social development as well as successful in neutralizing harmful media influences. Both restrictive and active mediation can diminish negative media effects such as the learning of violent behav-ior, substance use, and sexual conduct, according to a recent meta-analysis (Coyne et al., 2017). Parents who have little control over their children are more likely to allow their 10 or 11-year-olds to be exposed to excessive screen time. Whereas, parents like Georgia, who exercise greater control while remaining supportive of their children are more likely to employ active and restrictive mediation with their children aiding in overall development (Coyne et al., 2017). It is also important to emphasize that Georgia's children were raised in the late 1990's to mid-2000's where technology and media use was still emerging and not quite widespread as it is currently in 2023. Thus, her children not having a mobile phone for instance until age 15, may have been the likely norm at the time, also factoring in financial components of such purchases.

Georgia mentions how she encourages her children to be imaginative and play instead of relying on media, which is also supported by developmental theories examining its importance as well. Play is universal and strategies for spirited childhood sociality have existed in every society across time (Singh and Gupta, 2012). Childhood in most civilizations is heavily shaped by family values and societal ideas, which in today's world make up the overall educationally based communal definition of childhood. Yet, theorists such as Piaget, Erikson and Vygotsky believed that children utilize play to teach themselves and play through situations similar to adults thinking (Singh and Gupta, 2012). Through imaginative play, children learn to live within self-imposed boundaries, learn to represent ideas and objects through fantasy and practice self-regulation of distress (Singh and Gupta, 2012). Especially, outside play which is critical for a child's development, health and happiness. As children grow older, play becomes more complicated, allowing them to learn mastery and coordination. Play is viewed as learning in a less risky environment, with fewer repercussions of action and numerous possibilities to explore combinations of behavior that would not be tried otherwise (Singh and Gupta, 2012). Moreover, children can internalize and reflect cultural tendencies, patterns, and values through play. Role identity and cultural expression may be held together via play as well (Singh and Gupta, 2012). Parents that recognize the importance of play which includes physical activity, enjoyment, and an outlet for surplus energy are seen to have a more secure attachment. Thus, parental involvement and encouragement of play, creativity and imagination as Georgia mentions, provides a space for children to learn, grasp social roles, and enact hopes, worries and needs, resulting in a more developed and harmonious self-concept. Parental involvement, creativity and co-play, in some manner, is directly related to how Georgia motivates her children.

She shares that to help keep her children motivated, she maintains engagement and involvement with them. She states, her children were always with her doing whatever she was doing, ranging from cleaning to planting flowers in the garden to woodwork. She provided them with the space and materials to do art and be creative through anything they wanted, whether it was making costumes or cooking. She allowed them to work on things manually, get dirty out in the mud or rain, experience and create whatever and whenever they wanted to. According to Hawkins (2002), drawing or artwork is a child's spontaneous activity, a playful game, an escape, and, simultaneously, the exploration of total freedom that permits the expression of needs or wishes, as well as release from fears. This is why drawing, art and creativity play an important role in children's general education throughout their early years of school and are frequently employed as a psychotherapeutic approach when working with children. Art, drawing, and visual representation are seen to be ways for the inner self, cultural practices, and systems to be projected outwardly in the process of identity exploration and formation (Hawkins, 2002). In fact, art-based psychotherapies for families propose that the parent-child connection comprises distinct types of communication: explicit (i.e., conscious verbal language), implicit (i.e., unconscious processes of relationships and world) that can be concurrently and symbolically expressed through parents and children jointly expressing creativity together (Gavron and Mayseless, 2018). According to Parent-Child Art Psychotherapy, a revolutionary new inventive approach, the use of playfulness and imagination during joint parent-child art creation typically leads to the building of a unique narrative of the dyadic connection and permits communication that is not commonly transmitted orally and strengthening bonds and attachment (Gavron and Mayseless, 2018). Furthermore, Olszewski-Kubilius (2018) claims that parents transmit several messages and values to their children verbally as well as through actions, which are essential for a child's success. Values embodied by parents that encourage talent and achievement can include, among other things, the importance of being mentally curious or investigative, the significance of creativity and creative production, and the importance of active recreational quests—e.g., hobbies or having meaningful pursuits and so on (Olszewski-Kubilius, 2018). Modeling autonomous interests, self-study, self-efficacy, artistic interests, leisure reading and civic involvement are just a few examples of supportive measures that parents can demonstrate to their children for appropriate skill, talent and identity development, similar to what we can observe with Georgia (Olszewski-Kubilius, 2018). Now that her children are older, the eldest being 29, they still continue to make things with their hands. For example, her son skillfully made a bag using old clothes for her husband as a Christmas present. Her other son is talented in using logs from trees to carve bowls. She says, this is different to what she does, she cannot sew or create furniture, although she can fix furniture, but her children found their own unique ways to use art and express themselves through it as they grew older. Georgia providing the space, expressing freedom, value and joint connection through art has had significant influence on not only her children's ability to express or communicate themselves through non-verbal implicit means but also develop talented skills and integrate this as a part of their identity. All her children are very involved in art, music and expression till date, some taking on artistic career paths as well.

Georgia continues explaining obstacles she faced when parenting her children from a young age where she learned to avoid certain things such as a strict bedtime which most mothers in her children's preschool followed (e.g., putting the kids to bed at 7:00 PM). She never believed in it, she let the children nap in the afternoon which meant they were awake later at night. But, this worked well, as she wanted the children to go out with her to restaurants at night and be able to enjoy their time out, since they also did not have babysitters readily available. She tried the strict bedtimes for a short period with her first two children and then avoided it with her last two children. Oftentimes, she said, books would recommend strict bedtimes to help build structure for children, but she worked hard in finding another way that worked just as well for both herself and her children. Sleep expectations and perceptions of sleep issues or routines are influenced and differ according to cultural norms for both parents and healthcare workers (Mindell et al., 2013). Cross-cultural studies have found that there are vast differences in bedtimes and daytime sleep routines across countries/regions with the most striking insights according to Mindell et al. (2013), suggesting no differences in time spent sleeping across 24 hours for all children. Bedtimes in all countries in the study ranged from 7:43 P.M in Australia and 10:26 P.M in New Zealand and in India (Mindell et al. 2013). In comparison to Caucasian preschool children, who were no longer napping by this age, going to bed early in the evening and getting the majority of their sleep at night, the majority of children in Asian countries continued to nap into their preschool years and went to bed later at night; their sleep was divided between the day and night, but they got the same quantity of sleep as Caucasian children (Mindell et al., 2013). It seems understandable through a cultural lens why Georgia naturally swayed away from books with rigid sleep routine advice that did not account for cultural differences and worldviews, since she raised her children in Greece, a collectivistic world where mid-day 'siesta' naps and later bedtimes are a collective norm for adults and children. This was evidenced by Paraskakis et al. (2008) where they revealed that young adolescents in Greece show similar patterns of later bedtimes and an increase in midday naps compared to northern European or more Caucasian regions. Paraskakis et al. (2008) also shed light on midday naps being associated with a countries' geographical location being closer to the equator leading to warmer climates and light conditions. It is also postulated that midday naps are not correlated to night-time sleep disturbances nor with higher daytime sleepiness. Alternatively, it was found that midday naps with Greek adolescents minimized tiredness, boosted performance and preserved vigilance during the day (Paraskakis et al., 2008).

Therefore, it is observable that Georgia's parenting choices, in terms of sleep, are not seen as harmful, rather, they can be beneficial for children raised in Greece, following societal norms of functioning.

Recently, Georgia pursued a masters in Psychology in her 50's and perhaps, observing her as a role model, her youngest daughter Penny has also pursued a degree in Psychology simultaneously. Georgia explains how lucky she feels to have a good relationship with her children and being so emotionally connected to them. She emphasizes that being her true self is what led her to raise her children into the wonderful individuals they have become. She believed in herself and in how she wanted to raise her children, without over controlling them and just allowing them the freedom to choose. Additionally, she shares that children have to endure a strict academic world currently, especially in Greece, and she did not want her children to feel stressed in every aspect of the world without any liberty, especially at home. This is why she also emphasized a certain level of freedom and play, creating some balance.

Georgia shares stories of successes with her children which include all of her children having empathy for other students in school being bullied or if they were different. She shares an account of when one of her sons came home crying because another student had been put in the trash can in school and he tried to help by informing a teacher. On another occasion, her daughter brought home a friend who was really struggling with trauma and stood by her and supported her in any way she could. She felt proud knowing that her children were empathetic and compassionate to others and would go out of their way to aid others in need. Even when her children were being bullied themselves, especially her oldest two children, she shares that they did not alter themselves to change the circumstances, they stuck with who they truly were, accepted it for a while and found their way out of it, with the support of their friends. When children of authoritative parents are given difficult activities or are pushed to overcome obstacles, they exhibit perseverance and gain self-confidence, according to Baumrind (1967, 1971, 2005) as well as Kotaman (2013). The child's ability to overcome the problem will mark their achievement in a more meaningful manner leading to a sense of personal fulfillment, which is seen as an effective way to develop a sense of self and inner motivation. Finally, Georgia shares that the two things that make her feel she has been a successful parent is knowing her children stick to their values of love, care, compassion, helpfulness and empathy. She also shares that she is not a perfect parent nor a perfect person, but she has good children because they have a heart, they understand what is good in the world and embrace it and she couldn't be prouder. It is always interesting to hear how parents describe their children's successes, either by their academic or life achievements, or by how they view their parents or, as Georgia shows us, by who they are as people and how incredibly they demonstrate their values.

Penny, Georgia's daughter describes herself as creative, compassionate, trust-worthy, naïve and hard-working. She explains that she still has a lot to learn about the world since she grew up in a safe environment, which often makes her surprised or shocked hearing terrible things that are happening in the world, which is why she considers herself naïve but always welcomes becoming more self-aware about the world. She also feels that she is quite optimistic and always chooses to view the good side of situations or people without a second thought. Penny expresses that she stays motivated by engaging in projects or tasks that she enjoys. She is fond of brainstorming novel ideas or activities, discussing them with her peers, planning and researching her notions, all of which, as a process maintains her motivation. She expresses that money is not a motivator to her but having passion towards tasks she is pursuing is a larger motivator. Additionally, knowing that she will gain something personal from tasks, rather than materialistic gains, serves as a motivator as well. This goes hand in hand with the Self-Determination Theory that suggests, internal rather than external goal pursuits have more favorable outcomes on well-being (e.g., mental health) and education, according to Turner, Chandler, and Heffer (2009). Furthermore, this theory distinguishes three forms of motivation: Intrinsic Motivation—participating in a task based on pleasure and contentment from the process; Extrinsic Motivation—taking part in a task or activity to meet an external demand, or to achieve a reward such as money; and Amotivation—not being intrinsically or extrinsically motivated to do a task or activity. Penny describes being intrinsically motivated for tasks or activities as she enjoys the process of the task rather than the external rewards, this itself becomes fulfilling for her. Literature reveals that autonomy-supportive home environments increase intrinsic autonomous motivation, while controlling circumstances decrease such motivation (Turner, Chandler and Heffer, 2009). We can link this to Georgia's parenting approach of having her children participate in activities they appreciated and were passionate about which internally has become a motivator for all sorts of activities in Penny's life as an adult. Penny shares how growing up, her parents never really emphasized that she had to get good grades in school, they however, communicated that she should try her best and put in all top efforts, regardless of the outcome. They would praise her if the outcome was good, but they never forced her to get specific grades. She says that she was motivated by their encouragement and their support. Similarly, in school, teachers also encouraged creativity, curiosity and a drive for learning which motivated her further. Studies have found that children or students who felt that their parents promoted the development of effective communication abilities and independence, while still maintaining reasonable boundaries to operate within (i.e., authoritative parenting style) were more likely to succeed academically (Turner, Chandler and Heffer, 2009). Not only did these students have higher GPAs, but they also had stronger academic self-efficacy as well (Turner, Chandler and Heffer, 2009). Moreover, children whose parents were described as authoritative, such as Georgia, were the most motivated, capable and goal-oriented. In addition, authoritative parenting was found to be favorably connected with academic success across cultural groups in studies (Turner, Chandler and Heffer, 2009). Intrinsic Motivation and self-efficacy was again found contributing to academic success, in addition to the impacts of authoritative parenting on academic performance. Self-efficacy is described as the belief in one's ability to plan and carry out the actions necessary to achieve specific goals in a variety of situations, including conquering fears, achieving success in the work environments, navigating difficult life transitions, and academic performance/achievement (Turner, Chandler and Heffer, 2009). Research shows that authoritative (supportive) parenting approaches in a parent-child relationship predicts a child's sense of mastery (i.e., belief in controlling one's environment) early in life, building in internal motivation, self-confidence, self-esteem and self-efficacy (Turner, Chandler and Heffer, 2009). As we have reviewed Georgia employing such a parenting approach with Penny, the outcomes are evidently observable with Penny feeling a sense of efficacy when she tries her best on tasks without worrying about punishing or controlling consequences from her parents, being more internally motivated to focus on tasks that are meaningful and feeling a sense of reward from the process, whether it is academic or personal. It should also be noted that Penny is in good academic standing in her current college degree and shared similar achievements in school as well, corroborating past research.

She goes on to share lessons she would pass down to her children from her childhood which include finding your own happiness, a strong value system—knowing what is ethical and moral, not necessarily what is right, but rather what feels good to you. Additionally, being compassionate, which was an important lesson her parents taught her as well, which she appreciated. Penny's statements are directly mirroring Georgia's value system of being a good person morally, following one's heart and her prosocial behavior which was modeled to her children making them empathic, compassionate and proactive individuals, as seen with Penny and across literature. She would also like to maintain how her parents shared detailed aspects of their cultures and backgrounds with her and her siblings. She would aim to recreate a sense of openness with her children as her parents had with her. Once more, we observe an absorption, appreciation and mirroring of Georgia's value of being honest and open with oneself and others, as well as ensuring a sense of identity exploration by sharing cultural differences and similarities from her own experiences. These were effectively passed down to Penny in a positive light, driving an intergenerational cycle of affirmative traits, values, beliefs, thoughts to continue on from one generation to the next. However, Penny would change how her parents treated her and her siblings differently, not favoring anyone but, for example, allowing the youngest child less tasks/chores or responsibility at home. She would make sure when she has children that all of them have equal responsibility and consideration.

Penny also shared memories from her childhood that have played a role in shaping who she is presently. One of her memories involves spending time with her family every summer at Greek islands or visiting family in the U.S, as these experiences shaped how she views the importance of family, what a family is and what it means to have them as an unconditional support system. Other memories include being appreciative of having nature surrounding her and being able to go outside and play. Especially being in Greece, she feels grateful for nature and scenic environments. As we have explored the importance of play previously, it is important to emphasize once more that parents such as Georgia recognizing the influence of play on Penny's development and creating a space to reconnect with one's senses and the world, not only creates a more attuned secure attachment (Bowlby, 1969; Ainsworth, 1979) between Penny and Georgia, but also promotes learning mindfulness, happiness and forms of self-regulation (Singh and Gupta, 2012).

Penny also points out that each parent may describe success with their child very distinctly. In her case, her parents just wanted her to be happy, they viewed her contentment and overall positive well-being as a success to them. In her opinion, parents who want to raise their children to be successful, with similar values as her parents instilled in her, should incorporate qualities such as: motivating their children to engage in different activities that they enjoy (without being forceful) and being supportive of their choices, while being approachable for children to come talk to but also having certain boundaries to ensure a balance. Penny describes briefly characteristics of authoritative supportive parenting, which in her view allow for well-rounded successful children, however success may be defined subjectively for each individual.

STORY 4: CHRISTINA & LUCAS

Christina begins her interview by stating that she has two children; her son Lucas is 11 years old and her daughter is 9 years old. Christina is an educator, a teacher and what sparked her passion towards education as well as her inspiration behind her parenting approach was reading about alternative approaches that help children learn. One influential approach that interested her was experiential education, especially by Maria Montessori, who worked with orphan girls back in the 1800's to mid-1900's which has grown immensely in present day with the famous Montessori system schools found all over the globe. For context, the Montessori method treats children as whole beings with minimal adult intervention (Faryadi, 2007). Dr. Maria Montessori felt that each learner is a unique individual who has the ability to surprise us with previously undiscovered abilities. To completely develop the undiscovered, we must give them the freedom to explore their surroundings. We can help them by using sensory-based education methods which have been proven effective according to research, with several limitations as well (Faryadi, 2007). In other words, children are given a holistic approach status and rather than forcing children to study, this technique provides a sense of direction by adults. As a result, it is possible to gain the required skills to achieve academic success, a sense of mastery and competency in a learning environment through the use of play and sensory integration (Faryadi, 2007). Although we know from past research, the importance of play and incorporating sensory stimulation which is useful for a child's development as seen through research, the lack of adult intervention when it comes to child rearing practices can be similar to permissive parenting which views children as inherently capable beings, leading to additional consequences.

Christina explains that she has never been mainstream and likes to explore our internal world—understanding who she is. She is an open, inclusive person and enjoys meeting individuals from other cultures. She can be sensitive towards individuals who are new to a group and seeks to bring them into this internal world of hers in order to make them feel welcome. She discusses how this is linked to her growing up with parents from mixed cultures and being moved around, relocating across the world quite frequently, which has inspired her in a lot of different areas of her life. She grew up in the US for the first 5 years of her life, her mother is American with Italian descent and her father is Greek. She then came to Greece for about 4 years, she had to learn the language very quickly at age 5, but she enjoyed being surrounded by her extended family in Greece. At age 9, her family relocated from Greece again because work prospects were not great for her father, while her mother, she emphasizes, was a stay-at-home mom. They moved to Belgium, where Christina went to the European School in the English language section, after switching to Greek not so long ago. She felt that during this back and forth, she did not have a clear sense of her own identity which she struggled with for a long time. Growing up globally is not a novel phenomenon, but it is becoming more common in today's globalized world. The term "Third Culture Kid" (TCK) was coined by researchers to describe the many experiences of children who have led international lives unique from their home cultures, as well as the process of adaptation to a range of host cultures (Cockburn, 2002). A "Third Culture Kid," according to Pollock, Van Reken and Pollock (2010) describes someone who has spent a significant portion of their developing years outside of their parents' culture or in a cross-cultural mobile world.

TCKs are a broad category that includes expatriate children from all over the world, missionary children, military children, diplomat children, refugees, and other migrant children who live in a foreign culture (Cockburn, 2002; Miller, Wiggins and Feather, 2020). In terms of their educational, identity and cultural development, TCKs have had a one-of-a-kind experience. They frequently display adaptability and flexibility in their environment, yet they may fail to build a strong sense of self (Miller, Wiggins and Feather, 2020). Living in a third culture has a direct impact on a child's development as they are constantly exposed to different people, cultures and ideas without complete stability. Despite the fact that they form relationships with all cultures, they do not have full ownership of any of them (Cockburn, 2002). This is comparable to Christina's experiences and we may view her as a third culture kid who shares different cultural worldviews and experiences as she travels back and forth between cultures. According to the literature, TCK's like Christina experience extreme emotional turmoil as children as a result of repeated, frequently abrupt relationship shifts; safety and stability challenges in their environments; as well as the task of establishing an integrated and consistent sense of self-identity amongst so much change (Miller, Wiggins and Feather, 2020). This often leads to feelings of frustration, angst, emotional trauma, unresolved grief and lacking a sense of self (Davis, Edwards and Watson, 2015).

According to Erikson's (1963, 1968) psychosocial development stage model, adolescence is a difficult time for children as they struggle with identity and role confusion while attempting to discover their authentic selves. During this stage, young adults try to figure out who they are by engaging in various personal endeavors and experimenting with various roles (Erickson and Erickson, 1998; Miller, Wiggins and Feather, 2020). When adolescents complete this stage effectively, they should have a strong sense of self, are able to stay true to their views and ideals, and display a healthy personality which aids in overcoming potential crises (Erickson, 1963, 1968; Erickson and Erickson, 1998; Miller, Wiggins and Feather, 2020). If an adolescent does not successfully finish the stage, they may acquire a weakened sense of self and endure role uncertainty. Such people may feel anxious, insecure, and bewildered about their future, and they will likely suffer as adults without a distinct identity (Erickson, 1963, 1968; Erickson and Erickson, 1998; Miller, Wiggins and Feather, 2020). Furthermore, TCKs may modify their identities to fit the numerous school environments they attend and/or the country they live in, never really creating a personal identity. It is because of the inherent separation that comes with going into the new and unknown, constant transition is a danger to one's identity, belongingness and not feeling at home anywhere. Also mentioned was how vulnerable these individuals are to peer pressure, which can lead to unhelpful behaviors and feelings like anxiety, despair, isolation, and a negative self-image, which are all typical among TCKs (Miller, Wiggins and Feather, 2020). Additionally, TCKs frequently suffer with interpersonal communication and relationships, as well as personal wellness, which originates from a lack of identity, as a result of their constant mobility. TCKs are more likely to experience loneliness, depression, and other mental health issues if they do not have the opportunity to build trust in others and form meaningful relationships (Miller, Wiggins and Feather, 2020). The above literature provides a deeper understanding into the practical struggles and emotional as well as developmental challenges faced by Christina's continuous childhood relocation. Christina shares that when she finished school, she moved to the UK where she did her first degree and decided to go into teaching (both her mother and grandmother had also been teachers). To pursue teaching further, she went to New York at the age of 21, staying for 15 years and this is where she discovered who she was. She felt that the city and its environment was welcoming, providing a safe as well as stable space for her to explore herself and fully develop a firm sense of self internally and in-relation to her environment. Linking this to Christina's interest in the Montessori approach where environmental exploration through sensory means in order to gain a sense of mastery, safety and security seems understandable, given her experience from a young age of moving from location to location that did not allow for such meaningful environmental adaptation. This can be viewed as one way she chose to make sense of her childhood experiences and the world, while also gaining professional benefits as well. As we understand from Albert Ellis's ABC model and attachment bonds: during developmental years of our lives, we form beliefs of ourselves, others and the world, therefore, if Christina's world constantly changed, it can be assumed on the basis of research that her beliefs of herself as well as the world altered frequently leading to internal disconnect and attachment insecurity (Bowlby, 1969; Ainsworth, 1979; Ainsworth, Blehar, Waters and Wall, 2015).

She openly shares that the continuous moving from country to country and changing languages as a child was internally traumatic for her and had impacts on her as a person, but she surmounted it. She has always been interested in trauma personally and has been studying it to also complement her background in primary education. Additionally, she has turned to mindfulness, self-compassion and EFT (Emotional Freedom Technique) practices to help her cope and obtain positive subjective well-being. She tries to bring in all of these aspects of herself and her interests into her family environment as well. Mindfulness is defined as "the state of being attentive to and aware of what is happening in the present" in literature. Mindfulness meditation focuses on a variety of elements such as physical sensations, mental moods, and connections between one's behavior and the environment, and incorporates paying close attention to one's own personal experiences in order to create calmness and steadiness (Follette, Palm and Pearson, 2006). The content of thoughts and feelings is not disregarded, suppressed, scrutinized, or judged. Rather, as these events enter the field of awareness, they are registered as they occur and observed nonjudgmentally, bit by bit permitting individuals to "calmly endure" current circumstances (Follette, Palm and Pearson, 2006). Mindfulness Meditation is supposed to aid in the development of self-acceptance by fostering perseverance, awareness, readiness to experience emotional distress, and honing in on the present-moment. People who practice these activities in both pleasant and painful situations perceive themselves as part of a larger context, not as bad or good, but as part of a constantly changing cosmo (Follette, Palm and Pearson, 2006). This attitude towards life events is at the heart of several psychotherapeutic approaches including Acceptance-Based Therapy (ACT) and Dialectical Behavior Therapy (DBT). Studies claim that the ability to self-regulate one's behavior is connected to being mindful and increasing an individual's overall well-being (Follette, Palm and Pearson, 2006). Furthermore, mindfulness skills have shown to be an effective approach when working with trauma, in combination with other psychological approaches such as CBT. Using mindfulness as a coping tool for traumatic symptoms allows for skills training in affective, interpersonal and bodily regulation while increasing emotion control, resiliency, positive well-being and reducing anger, stress, grief, depression, post-traumatic stress symptoms as well as anxiety (Follette, Palm and Pearson, 2006).

Self-compassion is a multifaceted concept that has been shown in studies to improve well-being and lessen mental health issues. Self-compassion is a type of responsive self-relating marked by the ability to approach oneself with similar kindness and compassion as one would relay to others in similar circumstances (Winders et al., 2020). It entails a non-judgmental attitude toward oneself, seeing one's experiences as part of a greater human predicament rather than feeling isolated, increasing awareness of distressing experiences and engaging with them in a balanced and neutral manner without overidentification (Winders et al., 2020). Early childhood experiences that were stressful, frightening or lacked appropriate care, similar to the level of stress Christina felt during continuous life changes, leads to an underdeveloped self-soothing inner system and a hyper-aroused stress/threat system (Winders et al., 2020). Compassion, on the other hand, is a prosocial motivational system that is designed to regulate negative feelings by being aware of suffering in oneself and others, and making a commitment to alleviate it through emotions of warmth and safety (Winders et al., 2020). Self-compassion as a coping strategy for trauma, according to a meta-analysis of 35 studies by Winders, Murphy, Looney and O'Reilly (2020), lowers trauma symptoms and PTSD outcomes. It is also linked to adaptive coping techniques such as tackling difficulties head on, making reasonably realistic assessments of situations, identifying and modifying inappropriate emotional responses, and attempting to avoid negative bodily impacts (Winders et al., 2020). High self-compassion is linked to lower levels of avoidance, suppression of negative thoughts and rumination, as well as increased interpersonal connectedness. Increased self-compassion has been reported to reduce shame, negative self-evaluation, self-criticism, self-blame, and guilt, as well as diminish avoidance of emotional distress (all outcomes of trauma as well) (Winders et al., 2020). Combining Christina's practice of mindfulness with self-compassion would allow her to learn self-soothing strategies to manage emotional, mental as well as physical distress, while creating a safe and kind mental space to process events and build a healthy self-concept. Mindfulness and self-compassion go hand in hand, as mindfulness encourages self-acceptance and self-compassion is the specific tool that motivates such acceptance and this is often why it is incorporated in several psychotherapeutic techniques. Given her unstable developmental period as TCK; forming internal stability as a resource is extremely beneficial to increase feelings of control, confidence, joy and calmness.

Moreover, Christina also mentions the use of Emotional Freedom Technique (EFT) to cope with TCK related trauma. EFT is a psychophysiological strategy that incorporates aspects of Cognitive Behavioral Therapy (CBT), Exposure Therapy, and Somatic Activation through acupressure points, often referred to as "tapping" (Clond, 2016). Briefly, individuals use this method by choosing a distressing memory or experience, which is verbally recognized and reframed using a self-acceptance statement. The sentence is repeated 5 to 10 times while tapping with one's fingertips on 12 acupressure spots to maintain focus on the present issue and down-regulate the limbic system's activity (part of the brain involved in our behavioral and emotional responses, including the fight/flight response triggered during stress) (Clond, 2016). Research shows that this technique reduces blood flow in many brain regions related to memory and stress activity, decreasing stress-related cortisol and bodily symptoms of stress such as tension and headaches (Clond, 2016). It is likewise seen to reduce different forms of anxiety, including phobia related distress, while also being an appropriate regulating tool for individuals with trauma and PTSD. EFT is taught easily to anyone and is seen as a hands-on practical strategy for coping with emotions and learning to appropriately care for oneself (Clond, 2016). Therefore, Christina's use of EFT in combination with Mindfulness and Self-Compassion is one effective way of coping with emotional dysregulation, learning to tolerate distress, manage unresolved grief from multiple losses due to frequently mobility during childhood, increasing self-awareness as well as understanding and leading a more positive life mentally and physically (Davis et al., 2015). All of these methods in conjunction with her knowledge about trauma and psychology has been useful in her developing a healthy and informed sense of self. It should be emphasized that these methods are not an alternative for psychotherapy yet are used in combination with other effective approaches to enhance well-being.

Christina has replicated aspects of her own upbringing when raising her children, one of the most important facets includes being open and flexible. This was emphasized in her own life due to continuous relocations and was incredibly important to her to pass this down to her own children. Openness, she describes, can be experimenting or trying new experiences or new cuisines as a family, with the aim that her children and family unit can grow and expand together. This approach is heavily linked to supportive authoritative parenting practices that encourages creativity, problem-solving development, growth mindset (rather than rigid fixed thinking), autonomy and openness to experience as a trait. According to Neitzel and Stright (2004), there is a link between parent personality and chosen parenting practices based on those personality traits leading to child outcomes. One of the leading models of personality focuses on five major factors of personality: Neuroticism, Extraversion, Agreeableness, Openness to Experience and Conscientiousness (Neitzel and Stright, 2004). The Openness component of personality describes a person's attitude and response to new experiences. It includes active imagination, creative appreciation, responsiveness to inner feelings (both positive and negative), fondness for diversity, intellectual inquisitiveness, and freedom from judgment (Williams et al., 2009). Due to Christina's upbringing as a TCK and having to adapt to a diverse range of experiences, we can assume that she is high in the trait "Openness." Individuals like Christina, with a high level of Openness are often inquisitive and adaptable in their thinking with a diverse range of interests, are willing to try new things based on intellectual interests and creativity, and are sensitive to the inner moods and emotions (Neitzel and Stright, 2004). Parents with a high level of Openness aim for their children to share their enthusiasm for a variety of activities; are more likely to engage in instructional approaches like prompts, questions, and clues to enlist their children's active cognitive participation in the problem-solving process (Neitzel and Stright, 2004). Such joint problem-solving and shared experiences also demonstrates supportive co-regulation to children and maintain secure attachment in the parent-child dyad (Bowlby, 1969; Ainsworth, 1979). Openness as a trait is seen to be an important resource for parents as well when helping their children solve unfamiliar or tough problems, because providing high-quality support in the assistive instructional role requires parents to be interested in the child's role and responsive to their cognitive and emotional needs (Baumrind 1967, 1996, 2005; Neitzel and Stright, 2004).

Some academics describe Openness as intellectance, while others consider it to be more of an aspect of intelligence as well as personality (Dollinger, Leong and Ulicni, 1996). Furthermore, research by Koestner, Walker and Fichman (1999) implies that creativity and Openness to Experience may be strongly associated. The presence of three internal conditions is required for the formation of creative behavior: an internal locus of assessment (i.e., 'the value of the creative work is defined by oneself, not by the praise or criticism of others'), openness to experience (i.e., absence of rigidity and fluidity of boundaries in ideas, beliefs, perceptions, and hypotheses is referred to as openness to experience), and the ability to experiment with components and concepts (i.e. play intuitively with concepts, to juggle elements, to mold wild assertions and translate them from one form to another) (Koestner, Walker and Fichman, 1999). As a result, it is claimed that these three internal capacities are most likely to arise when individuals feel comfortable and free to express themselves in social settings while complementary research on imagination and creativity suggests that a pleasant, supportive environment that is largely free of restraints enables creativity (Dollinger, Leong and Ulicni, 1996). Thus, Christina providing the space to explore allows for the development of creativity, growth perceptions, inner trust, and autonomy in her children (Koestner, Walker and Fichman, 1999). Furthermore, Openness to Experience as a personality trait has recently also been recognized as a predictor of better health outcomes in chronic illness patients (Williams et al., 2009). Although the mechanisms behind these relationships still require further exploration, it is thought that Openness may protect individuals against the damaging consequences of stress. According to preliminary research, Openness is connected with cognitive abilities that access the dorsolateral prefrontal cortex patients (Williams et al., 2009). Complementary, recent models of self-regulation, such as the Neurovisceral Integration Model and the Polyvagal Theory, place a strong emphasis on prefrontal brain functioning managing and buffering detrimental effects of stress in trauma patients (Williams et al., 2009). Studies suggest that individuals with higher levels of Openness had a combination of increased parasympathetic response (i.e., the body's relaxing, rest and digest system involved in regulation), lower sympathetic reactivity (i.e., the body's stress activation system—fight/flight), and modestly significant improvements in positive feelings in the setting of a stressor patients (Williams et al., 2009). Similarly, Williams et al. (2009) found that individuals high in Openness are more stress resilient, while low-Open people are more vulnerable to the negative impacts of stress. Likewise, Balgiu (2017) postulated a relatively favorable link between personality traits, including Openness to Experience and Resilience. Consequently, we emphasize that Christina encouraging Openness to novel experiences with her children contributes to the development of resilience, self-regulation, positive well-being and stress management, linking to Masten and Monn's (2015) family resilience concept.

Christina shares that there are aspects of how her parents raised her that she is now aware of and decided not to replicate as a pattern with her own children. One of which she avoided was being overprotective of the children which to her leads to naivety and lack of independence. She says that, children nowadays are able to grasp things much faster and learn to be more precautious, children are not as naïve as we assume. She is not afraid to tell her children about things that are frightening and compassionately help them build their understanding of the world. Furthermore, Christina also chose to avoid putting excessive pressure/demands on her children, as her father put on her. She explains that when she was young, she felt like she had to be a specific way or do certain things, with stressful thoughts like 'I have to do this' without her parents considering how she felt about the task or activity. She remembers being taught to "complete tasks you dislike first and what you like last," which left her with the least amount of time to engage in activities she truly enjoyed. Through her personal growth and with the help of her husband, she has become aware of patterns from her childhood such as how she may unconsciously put pressure on her children to do what she thinks is good or correct without allowing her child to see how they feel about it. Thus, she asks her children for their thoughts and opinions, and she values how they feel about activities and works with them to find a middle ground. She teaches her children that their emotions, thoughts and feelings are valid and accepted in a give-and-take relationship and how to problem-solve as well.

According to Thomasgard and Metz (1993), parental overprotection is considered a form of restrictive controlling parenting practices, which we descriptively assume is an approach Christina's parents employed. Baumrind's (1971) typology may consider this forceful authoritarian parenting with high demand and low responsiveness to the child's needs. Authoritarian parents often do not appropriately communicate or explain why certain rules exist and nor do they provide reasons for their instructions to their children; they simply demand obedience without explanation and build distance between themselves and their children in order to protect their authority (Baumrind, 1971). As a result, they only communicate with their children on a limited basis. Facts of the world and rules are imposed onto children without having them put in self-effort to effectively understand why they must follow a certain path; this can lead to overcompliance (due to fear of being punished) and a lack of curiosity during developmental years (Kotaman, 2013). As we have examined, controlling parenting involves psychological and behavioral elements such as the management of children's behaviors through demands and rules, discipline through rewards and punishments as well as invasive control over a child's thoughts, emotions and beliefs (Kuppens and Ceulemans, 2019). Similarly, Thomasgard and Metz (1993) suggest that an overprotective relationship is defined by a parent who is: 1) extremely watchful and supervising, 2) has difficulty separating from the child, 3) discourages autonomous activity, and 4) is extremely controlling. Such "controlling" overprotective behaviors have been connected to adult outcomes of dysthymia and anxiety disorders in the overprotected youngster in retrospective investigations. Such practices do not allow children to meet developmental stages of exploration, experimentation, problem-solving, critical thinking, flexibility, independence/autonomy and are associated with insecure attachment styles (i.e., anxious, avoidant, fearful). Overprotective tendencies may be a reaction to untreated traumas in the parent's life, such as abuse, which has left the parent with a fear of the world (Thomasgard and Metz, 1993). Moreover, findings from studies suggest that parental trait anxiety paired with a lack of concern causes overprotective parenting. As a result, overprotective parents may overregulate their child's life and activities in response to their own internal uneasiness (Thomasgard and Metz, 1993). In contrast to an overindulgent parent-child interaction (where the attachment is often laced with guilt), clinical experience reveals that overprotective parents often develop an angry/hostile attachment to their child. The parent's ability to notice the child's separateness may be hampered by the attachment's profoundly ambivalent affects (Thomasgard and Metz, 1993). As Christina suggests, this form of parenting has several consequences including depression, anxiety, aggression, social avoidance, low self-esteem, deviancy, mental health struggles, lack of autonomy as well as identity and even emotional trauma (Kuppens and Ceulemans, 2019).

On the contrary, Christina's form of parenting takes on a more authoritative method which includes involvement, responsiveness and modeling for children's appropriate emotional regulation to cope with a variety of challenges (Baumrind, 1971; Kuppens and Ceulemans, 2019). Moreover, through this approach, parents orient children toward problems that are developmentally suitable, they do not employ punitive, harsh disciplinary tactics to guide their children; instead, they use demonstration, justification, reasoning, explaining, and monitoring to enable learning and develop critical thinking skills (Baumrind, 1967, 1971, 2005; Kotaman, 2013). Parents act as a catalyst in the development of their child's intellect and rationality, children's ideas, thoughts, and decisions are also respected and validated (Kudo, Longhofer and Floersch, 2012). They do offer protection, but in the form of supervision, so that children can engage in activities that will mold them, help them to learn and realize their full potential (Kotaman, 2013). Studies continuously reveal that the basis for a positive self-concept in children is based on early environments being open, understanding and collaborative (Kudo, Longhofer and Floersch, 2012). As a result, children who grow up in families where their parents treat them democratically—as a appreciated member of the unit with a participatory role—develop a positive self-image which aids in the development of a transformational leader (i.e., a leader who can inspire positive changes and has traits such as curiosity, energy, enthusiasm, confidence, empathy and passion) (Kudo, Longhofer and Floersch, 2012). There are three components of authoritative parenting which Kudo, Longhofer and Floersch (2012) point out and are worth emphasizing, they include: (1) nurturance and parent participation allowing children to be more open to parent influence; (2) a mixture of support as well as structure facilitates learning self-regulatory skills; and (3) the spoken give and take between a parent and child relationship absorbs the child in a process that cultivates cognitive and social skills while advancing behavior and emotion as well. The formation of emotional autonomy and mastery orientation in children are two key outcomes of authoritative parenting (Kudo, Longhofer and Floersch, 2012). Self-reliance, confidence, and a healthy sense of self are all products of emotional autonomy development. Mastery orientation allows a child to embrace difficult conditions and activities and eventually succeed through diligence, commitment and perseverance (Kudo, Longhofer and Floersch, 2012). As a result, children are also more securely attached to parents and are seen to have better overall psychological well-being as well as resilience throughout life. Therefore, Christina employing this form of parenting not only allows for her children to problem-solve and use their critical mind more readily, it also aids in development of communication skills, emotional distress tolerance, autonomy, self-confidence, self-efficacy, inner trust, solid sense of self, resilience, leadership skills, curiosity and regulation skills (Baumrind 1967, 1971, 2005).

Christina also chose to keep aspects from her childhood and her parents' approach such as cultural traditions and ways of being in the world. Her parents, she mentions, are from another generation which leads to a lot of differences between them. For example, she is much more open and comfortable to discuss topics of sexuality, however, her parents were more conservative when it came to this, as many people of their time. It is important to keep in mind that in certain cultures, such topics are not discussed with elders as they are considered taboo, inappropriate and disrespectful (Mulholland et al., 2021). Similarly, Maina, Ushie and Kabiru (2020) suggest that there are several variables, including parental shame when discussing sexual topics, cultural norms, and low self-efficacy, which consequently prevent parents from openly addressing sexuality-related matters with their children. Parental sharing of sexual and reproductive knowledge with their children may be hampered by a lack of sufficient and reliable sexual/reproductive information as well (Maina, Ushie and Kabiru, 2020). In a study with adolescents, Maina, Ushie and Kabiru (2020) found that a large percentage of young individuals expressed not having discussed sexual issues with their parents or not having meaningful, open dialogues about sexual matters that are important to their long-term health. It was discovered that these parents did not approve of romantic and sexual interactions for their children and frequently punished adolescents who engaged in such behavior (Maina, Ushie and Kabiru, 2020). Some parents never discussed sexual and romantic relationships with their adolescent children. Fear-based communication, supporting communication, or involving a third party (i.e., teacher or religious leader), were the three main tactics utilized by parents who attempted to discuss sexual health (Maina, Ushie and Kabiru, 2020). The primary purpose of parents initiating such conversations was to postpone romantic or sexual connections between young individuals, according to the study. It was seen that parents communicated to their daughters more than their sons and they often started conversations because something contextual (e.g., a young individual being pregnant in the neighborhood) had happened (Maina, Ushie and Kabiru, 2020). During these discussions, it was the parents who spoke in an authoritarian manner and made decisions for their children's sexual/reproductive health, making it a one-sided conversation (Maina, Ushie and Kabiru, 2020). Other studies support that parent-child communication on sexual and reproductive health (SRH) is critical in shaping what children believe, think, and practice with their sexual health, especially in the early stages of puberty (Mulholland et al., 2021; Maina, Ushie and Kabiru, 2020). Parents are seen as models for teaching behavior and understanding new developmental transitions based on the social cognitive theory, whereas in Bronfenbrenner's Ecological Systems Theory, parents are part of the micro-environment that influences a child's behavior directly and indirectly, this includes sexual health. According to some research studies, parent-child sex communication is highly linked to a child's safer sex practices, such as using condoms and delays in sexual activity. Yet, limited communication with parents was linked to less communication between young people and their sex partners, as well as reduced self-efficacy in negotiating safer sex practices (Mulholland et al., 2021; Maina, Ushie and Kabiru, 2020). Moreover, parental communication about this large aspect of a growing young adult's life increases parental bond, a sense of safety, self-confidence, connectedness and better psychological well-being while decreasing sexually risky behaviors, depression, anxiety, confusion and emotional distress. Christina being more authoritative and openly discussing topics such as sexual health when her children (without punitive measures) are curious provides the grounds for safer sexual behavior, security, sexual identity formation/exploration, overall increased mental health and secure attachment (Ainsworth, 1979). She also reduces stigma towards such topics indirectly when discussing them with her children.

Christina shares that overall, she felt there is a good balance in her current family. She married someone quite different to her father but there are lots of similarities as well. Additionally, the dynamic between her and her husband is very different to her father and her mother. She chose to uphold certain values from her family that include giving/sharing, family, empathy, not judging others and respecting elders—which is often emphasized in group-based cultures. However, values that are distinct from her parents that she feels strongly about involve taking care of yourself and the importance of dealing with difficult circumstances in a regulatory manner (as opposed to avoidance). She links this to an intergenerational belief that was bestowed onto her that "suffering is something that you must go through alone," but she feels that we are stronger with others. One can wonder if Christina's parents perceptions of suffering alone is linked to their migration journey—of being in several other countries and not having a sense of social embeddedness or connectedness to others leading to such a worldview which is distinct to how suffering is perceived in collectivistic cultures, as a group sharing pain together. Whereas, Christina finding a sense of community through her journey of exploring her identity as Third Culture Kid may have led to a change in worldviews. She also emphasizes similarly, that the value of community (i.e., we are better as a group than on our own) is extremely significant for her, revealing that she identifies herself with more collectivistic ideals in certain contexts. Other important values she upholds include respecting the environment, honesty, openness, communication, autonomy and independence which is revealed in how she parents her children.

Apart from her parents influencing her oppositional parenting approach, her life experiences and reading books by authors like Shefali Tsabary discussing "Conscious Parenting" are also significant factors. For context, Dr. Shefali Tsabary is a clinical psychologist who pioneered the paradigm Conscious Parenting in one of her bestseller books "The Conscious Parent: Transforming Ourselves, Empowering Our Children" (Tsabary, 2010). Conscious Parenting is a parenting style that focuses on the parent and how Mindfulness can influence parenting decisions. Instead of attempting to "fix" children, Conscious Parenting encourages parents to look inside themselves (Tsabary, 2010). Children can teach parents to become more self-aware through Conscious Parenting because they are independent beings (though they are still developing over time). Tsabary proposes that parents might begin to let go of their own checklists for how life should be lived by taking into account cultural and family inheritance and personal conditioning. Key elements of being a Conscious parent includes: viewing parenting as a two-way relationship, using self-reflection and eastern meditation practices to let go of parent ego, desires, and attachments instead of projecting them onto children; focusing on parental self-regulation and compassion to work through challenges; using appropriate boundaries and positive reinforcement instead of punitive disciplinary methods; understanding the roots of a child's behavior and gaining awareness; responding to child needs instead of reacting, and using mindfulness to continuously be present and engage with children from a place of acceptance (Tsabary, 2010). Likewise, Christina believes that she is learning from her children as much as they are learning from her. She mentions how she has grown up always striving to be the normative "good girl" defined by others and she is trying to break this pattern not only for herself but for her children too. She believes that her own internal growth and development has in-turn influenced her as a parent. This is understood by recognizing how individual change affects her as a mother since being a parent is not independent from past experiences, history, and individual identity. Rather, they are interconnected in a way that makes individuals whole, like a catalyst altering perceptions of one element affects others in this delicate ecosystem.

One of her aims as a parent is to encourage her children to feel independent and strong. She encourages her children to share their opinions and thoughts openly, making them feel included in the decision-making process—reflecting her supportive authoritative approach discussed previously. For example, she mentions planning a birthday party together with her children and teaching them how to cook meals for themselves on their own. Another important aspect Christina tries to instill in her children is being in-touch with their body. Instead of asking her children 'are you hungry?' she asks them 'what does your body need right now?' Given Christina's interest in mindful mind body practices, she enables her children to learn bodily awareness, attunement and regulation through eastern meditative methods. It should be mentioned that such forms of mindful awareness has been related to increases in psychological well-being and decreases in anxiety, stress and other mental health struggles including trauma (Follette, Palm and Pearson, 2006).

Christina discusses that there are different methods to keeping children motivated as each child is different and unique and no one size fits all. With her youngest child, she tries to break down unpleasant or difficult tasks to make it more manageable, disregarding the feeling that there is a mountain to climb. She feels that her open communication and exploration of challenges with her children (i.e., she talks to them about their thoughts and feelings) and searching for the root cause of their fears is helpful, as this is what blocks motivation. According to research, autonomy-supportive home situations boost intrinsic autonomous motivation (Turner, Chandler and Heffer, 2009). As discussed previously, children with authoritative parents as Christina were seen as intrinsically motivated, competent, goal-driven and academically more successful (Turner, Chandler and Heffer, 2009). Christina discusses going through a process of acknowledging and validating the fearful emotions with her children for them not to feel a sense of loneliness, allowing the emotion to dissipate with time and teaching them tolerance of unpleasant sensations. This inevitably gives them a sense of freedom and shifts their outlook on the situation, bringing back that lost motivation. The method Christina uses involves guiding her children compassionately to tolerate distress and self-regulating via communication, support, nurturance and mindfulness. Compassion itself is a motivational system that is aimed to regulate negative sentiments by being aware of suffering in oneself and others and committing to alleviating it through warm and safe emotions (Winders et al., 2020). Increased Self-Compassion has been shown to decrease shame, negative self-evaluation, self-criticism, self-blame and avoidance of emotional pain which often are demotivators, thereby increasing motivation and self-efficacy as well (Winders et al., 2020). According to studies, being aware and boosting general well-being are linked to the ability to self-regulate one's behavior (Follette, Palm and Pearson, 2006). Mindfulness meditation focuses on a variety of elements, including physical sensations, mental moods, and connections between one's behavior and the environment, and includes paying close attention to one's own personal experiences in order to self-soothe and feel a sense of calmness restored (Follette, Palm and Pearson, 2006). This is exactly how she teaches her children to cope with demotivation and any form of distress, boosting overall well-being and creating an alternate, more refreshed state of mind. She believes that verbalizing the emotion, getting in touch with thoughts and the body, creating this connection of self-awareness is invaluable when feeling down or demotivated. According to research, authoritative (supporting) parenting styles in a parent-child connection influences a child's sense of mastery (i.e., belief in managing one's environment or tasks), as well as motivation, self-confidence, self-esteem, and self-efficacy (Turner, Chandler and Heffer, 2009). Therefore, a combination of Christina's parenting practices all serve as forms of motivation as well. She also shares that she used to scream quite often before, not at her children but at her husband, and she has used mindfulness to transform that aspect of herself. It is important to note that Christina yelling or screaming could have been an old manner of regulating or tolerating uncomfortable emotions or stress that emerged, and through mindfulness she was able to find alternate self-soothing ways of tolerating such emotions. As research has revealed, mindfulness is an appropriate self-regulatory tool often used in psychotherapy as well.

Christina shares that she recognizes she is not a perfect parent, but she is always trying her best to grow and evolve and for her, that is a huge success as a parent. Finally, she shares a recent story where she felt like a successful parent, she describes that her son has some difficulty managing change. One day, in the car, she was saying to her son that she doesn't know which way to go while driving. To her surprise, he said to her "don't worry, just go with the flow." For her, this little moment was incredible because her son replicated or mirrored back to her the mindfulness practices she continuously repeated to help him, to be flexible and flowing in each moment. It filled her with hope that this practice might stick with them and help them in the future; a small but meaningful victory.

In our short interview with Lucas, who is 11 years old, he described himself as energetic (likes bicycling), social, funny and easily annoyed by his sister. To the question, "what motivates you and how do you stay motivated," he responded that usually he sets a reward for himself to obtain after he completes a task which helps him stay motivated (e.g., watch a video, go meet a friend). Lucas describes using extrinsic motivation based on gaining a reward for completing a task which might be used more currently based on his age as intrinsic motivation may be employed at a later developmental stage (Turner, Chandler and Heffer, 2009). As he shares a significant memory that shapes who he is, he discusses how he was scared of moving to a new school recently where he did not know anyone or where anything was. But, his teacher came to show him where his class was because he was lost. This was a big memory and moment because this teacher made him feel safe in an unfamiliar world and not so alone. Lucas mirrors Christina's value of community to help work through challenges as a team, rather than feeling a sense of loneliness and suffering alone. This is also significant of Lucas learning a sense of cultural identity to belong to a group with help, even when in an unfamiliar situation, such as a new school. For the next question, "which lessons from your parents are you going to pass down to your future children, and would you do anything different?," Lucas mentions how he likes that his parents are not very overprotective, he is allowed to go out alone by himself over small distances and they let him have an emergency phone which helps him feel independent and autonomous. He mentions how he also appreciates his parents organizing several different activities outdoors each week that are separate from school that engage the entire family. He explains that it is nice to get out of the house for activities other than school and having a good time. He would keep both these aspects from his parents when raising his own children. He doesn't think he would change anything for now.

Although Lucas is quite young, it is insightful observing his appreciation of the balance between independence, engagement and support received by his parents. Moreover, it is important to emphasize that Lucas was quite emotionally expressive, calm and self-reflective for a young child, which one could link to Christina's open, mindful and emotionally supportive parenting.

STORY 5: LISA & STEFANIE (CHILD ROLE)

Lisa, who is Italian and over 70 years old begins the interview discussing the inspiration behind her parenting approach. She mentions that more than anything, she raised her children based on her instincts and intuition. Lisa focuses on an interesting concept—Intuition—which is one that requires further exploration and emphasis when exploring parenting. Intuition is important in many aspects of life as it is becoming widely considered as a major mental faculty that plays an important role in exploration, problem solving, and decision-making, as well as a source of novel creative ideas, a predictor and disclosure of truths (Green, 2004). It is also recognized as a key part of wisdom, security, expertise, and creativity, all of which are important parenting attributes (Green, 2004). In Western culture, empirical data is recognized as valuable (i.e., logical reasoning based on facts) and important, while intuitive understanding is frequently undervalued. Philosophers such as Plato, Spinoza and Bergeson were the first to discuss "intuition" (Green, 2004). Moreover, in the field of psychology, Carl Jung described *Intuition* in his theory of personality, suggesting it is a psychological mechanism that conveys perceptions in an unconscious manner. Intuition, he said, is a process that unites the other psychological functions of sense, thinking, and feeling, and is necessary for survival (e.g., internal knowing when to flee a situation at signs of potential threat) (Green, 2004). Research also finds that implicit learning offers a nonconscious cognitive foundation for intuition, thus individuals have an instant emotion or judgment but are unable to explain exactly what they are basing that judgment on (Green, 2004). Therefore, intuition can be possibly viewed as the subjective experience linked with the utilization of knowledge learned through implicit learning. Wisdom includes intuition and wisdom is an important feature of parenting. Parents who have a good sense of judgment find it easier to raise children (Green, 2004). In cross-sectional studies across cultures, wisdom was defined by Eastern participants from collectivistic cultures as the successful integration of many facets of human consciousness (e.g., cognition, affect, intuition) (Green, 2004). Collectivistic group societies, according to this study, have already recognized the potential utility and worth of intuition, as we can also observe with Lisa.

Parenting concerns about safety and well-being are common across the globe. Intuition according to literature is also the backbone of safety. Even the word "intuition" comes from the Latin word *tuere,* which means to guard or protect (Green, 2004). Parents are continuously assessing situations to safeguard their children's well-being and safety. Parenting decisions such as these are critical (Green, 2004). Intuition can be a valuable tool in assisting parents with these issues. Moreover, creativity is said to be aided by intuition. It is suggested that creativity is an aspect of intuition, as creativity appears spontaneously with unique and valuable ideas (Green, 2004). Dreams, visions, and intuition have played a role in many of our cultures' creative successes, but modern society generally dismisses these experiences. Research by Heinberg cited Isaac Newton, Thomas Edison, and Albert Einstein as examples of such accomplishments (Green, 2004). Each of these men built something based on their instincts. Einstein frequently emphasized the value of intuition and he defined his own theories as a free invention of the imagination (Green, 2004). Parents may also find themselves in situations requiring innovative thinking. Some individuals consider intuition to be authoritative knowledge: understanding that it is used to make judgments and take action, which can be linked to specific parenting approaches as we have discussed in depth previously (Green, 2004). Intuition also influences educational practices in both teachers and parents like business, morality, emotional intelligence, nursing, medicine and counseling.

Counseling is incorporated into numerous parts of parenting. Children frequently seek assistance or advice on a variety of topics, and parents frequently listen, support, and offer suggestions (Green, 2004). Some people feel that Intuition has a place in counseling, and is potentially beneficial in parenting as well, given the similarities between parenting and therapy (Green, 2004). According to a study by Green (2004) examining parents' perceptions of the use of intuition in parenting practices, intuition was mentioned as quite valuable in assisting parents in making better decisions. Intuition is an untapped resource for parents resulting from a combination of tangible information, past experiences, the capacity to identify tiny hints and an indefinable emotion or subconscious sense (Green, 2004). The parents in this study felt that intuition can help promote their children's emotional and physical health. Examples mentioned about when intuition was prompted include situations where a child may be ill or during safety concerns, parents seem to piece together signals to diagnose the sickness and determine what type of care the youngster requires or does not require (Green, 2004). Intuition played a role in everything from picking a caretaker for an infant to deciding whether an adolescent could stay the night at a friend's home (Green, 2004). Intuition can also be used to predict what a child will do in a given situation and overall, aids parents in anticipating events, being more sensitive, assessing safety, and recognizing nonverbal clues (Green, 2004). Based on this in-depth exploration of intuition and parenting, it may be more understandable based on culture, past experiences and inner sense. Lisa's statement of using intuition is a major influence in her parenting approach.

Lisa shares that she did not raise her children in a similar manner to how she was raised because the circumstances were different including her parents being divorced. Her father was a very traditional Sicilian, who was 24 years older than her mother. Her mother was approximately 18 when she had Lisa. After her parents got divorced, WWII took place where Italians in certain regions (at the time, her father resided in Egypt) were being taken into concentration camps which inevitably was a consequence her father faced as well. This forced Lisa to live with her grandmother for security who raised her for a portion of her childhood. Civilians, women, children and society are inevitably affected by wars which are responsible for some of humanity's greatest pain and trauma (Osofsky, 2018; Waddoups, Yoshikawa and Strouf, 2019). Children who are directly or indirectly exposed to a war face a multitude of stressors and many of them suffer both short and long-term post-traumatic stress reactions which is known as War Trauma and Adverse Childhood Experiences (ACEs) (Felitti et al., 1998; Osofsky, 2018). Exposure to physical, emotional, and sexual abuse; emotional neglect; family dysfunction, including mental illness, war, natural disasters, racial/discrimination struggles, separation, death or loss of loved ones, community violence, divorce, domestic violence, incarceration of a household member, and substance misuse, are all examples of ACEs (Felitti et al., 1998; Osofsky, 2018). When young children are exposed to trauma, such as being separated from their primary caregivers, their ability to trust others is jeopardized (Osofsky, 2018; Waddoups, Yoshikawa and Strouf, 2019). Furthermore, if they are the victim or witness of violence or such as a painful separation—the results will be harmful for the young individual, leading to emotional and behavioral dysregulation (Osofsky, 2018; Waddoups, Yoshikawa and Strouf, 2019). Early investigations during WWII revealed an unusual finding in children who were separated from their parents and moved to rural locations to be protected from the dangers of war, such as Lisa. For these children, research found that separation from their parents was found to be more emotionally draining than the stressors of war; being separated from parents was far more difficult and traumatic (Osofsky, 2018). With political struggles such as war and society conflicts, both parent and child experience separation trauma, which may cause the parent to become more protective or hesitant being too close (Osofsky, 2018; Waddoups, Yoshikawa and Strouf, 2019). As a result, these attachment disruptions were identified as a critical factor of emotional and behavioral consequences in children (Osofsky, 2018; Waddoups, Yoshikawa and Strouf, 2019).

There are various sorts of parent-child separations, according to Waddoups, Yoshikawa and Strouf (2019) including being abandoned or orphaned in institutions, child trafficking and children who are left behind. Involuntary parent-child separation is a common cause of left-behind children and it is often the outcome of the trauma and instability connected with war, migration, and conflict (Waddoups, Yoshikawa and Strouf, 2019). In these situations, parents frequently leave their children with a caretaker, like with Lisa who grew up with her grandmother. The negative impacts of being abandoned by migrating or separated parents can be mitigated by a number of variables, the most important of which includes positive relationships with others or with the missing parents (Waddoups, Yoshikawa and Strouf, 2019). Studies suggest that a teacher-student connection, for example, positively predicted self-esteem and adversely predicted depression and problem behaviors in a sample of left-behind adolescents (Waddoups, Yoshikawa and Strouf, 2019). Friendship companionship for left-behind youngsters was also found to be favorably associated, in another study (Waddoups, Yoshikawa and Strouf, 2019). In Lisa's case, the open and free relationship with her grandmother could mitigate stressors of war and being separated from parents, promoting some level of resilience. However, it is important to note that inconsistencies or disruption/loss of key attachment relationships can still possibly lead to insecure attachment bonds in the future leading to emotional, cognitive and behavioral consequences.

The unique perspective and history that each parent contributes to their parenting practices is often overlooked while studying parent-child interactions. The experiences of a parent can have a significant impact on their parenting style and their children's growth (Treat et al., 2019). According to studies, parents' unfavorable childhood experiences have an impact on parenting, particularly among disadvantaged households (ACEs) (Felitti et al., 1998). Several studies, for example, have found that traumatic life events like child abuse and child sexual abuse have a negative impact on later parenting behaviors such as parental control and negativity (Treat et al., 2019). Increased stress, role reversal, permissive parenting, reduced perceived capability as a parent, decreased use of effective parenting approaches, parental animosity and the use of harsh physical discipline have all been associated with adverse early life experiences as well (Vafaeenejad et al., 2019). In other words, a history of child abuse can leave an imprint on a child's development that can continue into adulthood. Insecure attachments may be a risk factor for future parenting and impair positive parenting abilities as well (Vafaeenejad et al., 2019). However, much of the research on parent trauma and parenting behavior has focused on mothers who have been sexually abused or who are currently experiencing domestic violence (Riser, 2009). This limits our understanding about different sorts of traumatic experiences in a parent's past, such as war or separation, that may result in varied results for parents and have distinct effects on parenting habits (Riser, 2009). Monitoring and control are seen as negative parenting approaches with authoritarian patterns, however, positive child monitoring, may also be linked to a lower risk of children being exposed to some traumatic experiences, based on the parent's experiences (Riser, 2009). In Lisa's case, it can be assumed that due to the disruption in attachment and experiencing adverse experiences of war and separation had some effect on her parenting approach. As we will examine below, Lisa employs authoritative and some controlling authoritarian practices as well, taking into account the era she was parenting in, some practices were a part of the norm.

Lisa's grandmother was quite liberal for the era, making it not a very strict environment to be raised in. One can assume that her grandmother employed a more permissive parenting approach. On the contrary, Lisa was stricter with her two children, Paul and Stefanie. She was stern when it came to certain values such as good manners, nutrition, health and education—these are aspects of sociability and survival where parents may enforce certain rules to ensure their children are healthy mentally and physically. She mentions how her oldest, Paul was more indifferent, advanced and adaptable compared to his younger sister, Stefanie. She shares a memory of Paul when he was 16 years old where he was quarreling with his sister (also in her adolescence) and Lisa decided to intervene to guide her children on how to solve the dispute. Her children informed her that the conflict was between them and that they could resolve it on their own. She states, since that day, she has not interfered between them and has allowed them to tackle their own battles which they have effectively accomplished for years while maintaining a positive relationship till date. Studies have looked at process variables, such as parent–child interactions, as enabling positive child and adolescent sibling relationships (Milevsky, Schlechter and Machlev, 2011). Attachment and social learning theories propose that maternal responsiveness serves as an internal function, or social model for the child, that generalizes to other relationships, leading to expectations of consistent patterns of warmth across parent-child and sibling interactions (Milevsky, Schlechter and Machlev, 2011). Parents can play a crucial role in resolving conflicts between siblings by acting as a mediator and by encouraging family fairness standards and lowering dispute tension (Milevsky, Schlechter and Machlev, 2011). However, Adlerian theories postulate that sibling disputes are an attempt to attract parental attention and that involvement may increase future sibling antagonism. Past literature suggests that direct intervention tactics (i.e., coaching, mediation) used by parents were linked to reduced sibling intimacy and increased sibling negativity (Milevsky, Schlechter and Machlev, 2011). Studies observed that maternal non-involvement was connected to a higher level of sibling intimacy overall. Based on this, it is suggested that when parents feel confident that their children have a healthy relationship and can handle the situation on their own, they may choose to not become involved in sibling conflicts, this was certainly observed in Lisa's situation (Milevsky, Schlechter and Machlev, 2011. During this age, young adults begin exploring their independence, autonomy and work on enhancing their problem-solving skills, therefore, allowing them the space to resolve relational obstacles on their own without parental influence may be vital for their development into self-sufficient adults. Moreover, Milevsky, Schlechter and Machlev (2011) found that sibling support was higher among adolescents with authoritative and permissive parents than among those with authoritarian and neglectful parents. Children of authoritative parents also reported having closer sibling relationships than those with authoritarian or neglectful parents. Authoritative supportive parenting promotes socioemotional development in a variety of ways, with studies indicating that secure attachments and social learning, as well as tenderness, non-punitive approaches, and consistency, all linked to closer sibling relationships as well (Milevsky, Schlechter and Machlev, 2011). Lisa displays characteristics of authoritative parenting (i.e., high demand and low responsiveness) which could have contributed to her children having a close and positive sibling relationship (Baumrind, 1967, 1971, 2005).

Lisa mentions having specific rules for her children which was useful as they were growing older, one of them includes: they had to be home by 12 on Saturdays as long as they were still in school and she wanted to be informed when they left or returned home as well. She emphasizes that this was the beginning of the 80's when staying out late was becoming more popular. Additionally, for context, in the mid-80's and early 90's, late nights became a norm with late night discotheques growing across the globe. Although Lisa employs parental control and monitoring, which is most often viewed as an authoritarian approach, it can also be viewed as an authoritative approach where she respects her children's individual self-requiring independence and freedom by going out and being social, yet she also sets limits with supervision rules to ensure their safety (Baumrind, 1967, 1971, 2005; Kotaman, 2013). As we discussed previously, a balanced amount of parental monitoring through supervision, in circumstances, is seen as a positive practice of involvement/engagement, structure, decrease in risky or impulsivity, warmth, security and support (Riser, 2009). This is distinct to negative controlling parenting approaches as authoritarian parents exercise excessive control and do not accept children's autonomy or freedom (Kotaman, 2013). On the contrary, research has revealed that deficient control such as lack of attention, supervising and engagement with a child has been linked to the rise of mental health concerns like depression, anxiety and increased misbehavior (Kuppens and Ceulemans, 2019). Moreover, it is important to not discount that during this era in the early 1980's, children staying out late was still a new concept that parents were learning to adapt to, thus a specific curfew may have been the norm to cope with the changing world. Additionally, parental supervision to ensure security and safety may also be linked to collectivistic cultures being focused on the survival and safety of the group as well as family.

An additional value she upheld for her children included honesty, respect and good manners. She expresses that it was upsetting when her children lied and she recalls a time when her son had lied and forged her signature as a teenager. She states that she used slight physical punishment to discipline him. Lisa employed a form of controlling parenting to discipline her son during this instance through the use of physical punitive discipline (Kuppens and Ceulemans, 2019; Kotaman, 2013). This form of behavioral control is linked to negative emotional, psychological and behavioral consequences on the child. Although a youngster was more likely to comply with parental expectations immediately after being physically disciplined, researchers found that he or she did not develop the necessary good behavior or learning, thus making it a short-lived compliance with no long-term benefits (Elliman and Lynch, 2000). While not all children experience long-term unfavorable effects as a result of corporal punishment, studies found that the negative consequences of corporal punishment outweigh the ostensibly good short-term repercussions (Elliman and Lynch, 2000). The use of corporal punishment is linked to considerable increases in physical abuse, long-term antisocial behavior, anxiety, depression, low self-esteem, substance use and later abuse of a partner or child as an adult, as well as significant reductions in positive outcomes such as moral reflection, learning, awareness and empathy (Elliman and Lynch, 2000). Lisa states that this must have been her son's rebellious phase that most teenagers go through when trying to develop personality and autonomy. While in the 1970's and 80's corporal discipline was more prominent, this was a different generation with views and insights on discipline based on the generation prior to them, making this an intergenerational learning either through first-hand experience or observation. What makes this interesting is that Lisa employs certain authoritative practices within an authoritarian parenting style, making her parenting approach a combination of both. We were unable to locate past research on parenting combining parenting styles by each parent instead of strictly following one, this could possibly be explored in future research examining its effects on children. Although, it may be plausible that due to Lisa using a combination of parenting styles, the attachment styles occurring in her children could be a form of insecure attachment (i.e., avoidant or anxious). We point this out based on Ainsworth (1979) and Bowlby's (1969) studies suggesting that caregivers who are inconsistent, unpredictable and/or continuously changing may lead to children feeling anxious about how to navigate the caregiver.

Moreover, Lisa shares that she was not involved in motivating her daughter Stefanie for activities, tasks or her career choices from her adolescence onwards. She states that her daughter was her own self, she showed signs of knowing what she wanted to do (either in activities or in-relation to career goals), was autonomous, organized, determined and motivated from a young age. According to the literature, autonomy-supportive home situations boost autonomous motivation, whereas controlling conditions lower it (Turner,

Chandler and Heffer, 2009). Similarly, supporting parenting styles in a parent-child interaction influences a child's sense of mastery earlier in life (i.e., belief in managing one's environment), as well as motivation, self-confidence, self-esteem and self-efficacy (Turner, Chandler and Heffer, 2009). This could have been the case with Lisa's daughter and her choice in allowing her daughter to explore goals or tasks independently could have been a necessary space needed for her daughter to learn self-efficacy, face obstacles, develop problem-solving skills and resilience. However, research also claims that children whose parents reacted to academic grades with extrinsic rewards, punishments or stayed uninvolved, put in less effort in school and were less motivated (Ginsburg and Bronstein, 1993). Additionally, parental actions and family styles that were restricting of a child's independent thinking and conduct, critical or punishing, or even uninvolved, were projected to be connected with a more extrinsic motivational orientation based on developmental and social psychological theories (Ginsburg and Bronstein, 1993). Therefore, it is also plausible that Lisa being uninvolved in motivating her daughter could have been a factor that led to extrinsic motivation orientation relying on external rewards. Schooling could also be a factor in extrinsic motivation, creating space where students rely on examination results to move onto the next grades or receiving praise from teachers. In the last decade, cross-cultural motivation research has found that individualistic societies are more likely to identify intrinsic motivation with individual choice, curiosity, diversity, interest, and advancement incentives like the desire to grow or expand (Hennessey et al., 2015). Intrinsic motivation in collectivist cultures is often tied to the counsel of close friends or respected authorities, as well as preventative goals geared at preserving work or personal security (Hennessey et al., 2015). Moreover, it is vital to emphasize how societal gender roles and norms often play a role in accustoming women to grow up in a more self-sufficient manner, to consider thinking about their future from a much younger age and plan ahead of time, especially in the 1970's. This often has benefits as well as consequences to it.

However, with her son, Lisa was more involved, especially when he was in school, since he could not concentrate easily. She was involved in his studying process until he was 13–14 years old. Several studies have shown that parental involvement in children's education has favorable impacts across a wide range of communities and ages (Grolnick and Farkas, 2002). Parent involvement is defined as a parent's "commitment to his or her duty as a parent and to the nurturing of optimal child development" (Grolnick and Farkas, 2002). Parent involvement includes participating in school activities/conferences, engaging in activities at home such as homework, assisting in the selection of courses, keeping abreast of academic progress, reaction to academic grades, imparting parental values (attitudes about the importance of hard work and achievement) or amount of parental control or independent support available at home (Gonzalez-DeHass, Willems and Holbein, 2005). Literature suggests that when parents demonstrate an interest in what their children are learning, they establish a home support system that bolsters the child's academic learning and reaffirms the value of schooling. Parents provide the groundwork for socializing their children's motivation to learn by offering such emotional support (Gonzalez-DeHass, Willems and Holbein, 2005). The importance of education may be conveyed to the child as a result of the parent's involvement which may lead to more responsible and autonomous behavior at school (Grolnick and Farkas, 2002). Another factor to consider is the child's attitude toward oneself. A child who believes his or her parents to be involved, for example, may feel more capable. Involvement may also have a direct impact on accomplishment by assisting with studies and stimulating higher competence (Grolnick and Farkas, 2002). Furthermore, children in studies have reported higher effort, concentration and attention when their parents are participating. Children are naturally more interested in studying and have more internal motivation as well (Gonzalez-DeHass, Willems and Holbein, 2005). Extrinsic motivation is associated with parental homework supervision and the usage of extrinsic rewards in response to grades, but intrinsic motivation is tied to providing encouragement and praise (Gonzalez-DeHass, Willems and Holbein, 2005). Parents can also establish limits, provide support, and act as resources for their children as they face the academic, social, and personal obstacles that each new day brings. Parental participation shows children how valuable they are to their parents as well (Grolnick and Farkas, 2002; Gonzalez-DeHass, Willems and Holbein, 2005). This assistance is especially important for adolescents who are at danger of dropping out of school. Parental involvement may be more beneficial to a child's academic success when it occurs within an authoritative parenting style characterized by parental acceptance and warmth, as well as behavioral supervision that allows for some degree of democracy and autonomy for the child and their behaviors. This decreases behaviors such as absence, drug use, depression, poor grades, poor attendance, school disciplinary problems, and dropout (Gonzalez-DeHass, Willems and Holbein, 2005). Based on the above literature, Lisa's involvement with her son's schooling until adolescence was a way of increasing intrinsic motivation, sense of capability and mastery, self-confidence, achievement and maintaining secure attachment bonds by displaying her commitment to him. She also uses an authoritative supportive approach with high responsiveness and care while he faces such obstacles. Following her son's school years, Lisa was still involved in helping Paul pursue his chosen career; he had always wanted to be a pilot. She shares the story of how he achieved his dream—they had bought an encyclopedia one day which had some coupons and flyers within it. They looked into some information on these leaflets by calling to inquire about schooling in the UK until they found the Oxford Flying School, where Paul trained for 14 months and has been a pilot for major airlines ever since. One can wonder if Lisa's dedication to her son's achievement allowed him to gain confidence and intrinsic motivation to pursue goals and achieve career successes.

Finally, Lisa shares two memories where she felt she was a successful parent. For her daughter, it was watching her graduate with a degree from Scotland. For her son, it was at his graduation ceremony in Kidlington, Oxford where the instructor was sharing how good her son was at flying, especially, being so young. She was very proud of them and proud of who they continue to be.

Stefanie, Lisa' daughter who is in her 50's is also a mother, therefore, there are two different interviews with her below, one as a daughter and the other, *story 6*, as a mother. Her first interview begins with her describing herself as anxious, organized, slightly controlling, open and loyal. Note, aspects of this align similarly to how her mother describes her as a teenager. She describes, she stays motivated by looking at the bigger picture and thinking about what she will gain or achieve (e.g., money, gaining knowledge) when she completes an unpleasant task. She looks at the end goal which keeps her motivated to push further. Stefanie describes being extrinsically motivated—doing something as a mere means to meet an external demand or to earn a reward (Turner, Chandler and Heffer, 2009). In simpler words, extrinsic motivation is the desire to accomplish something in order to achieve a goal or meet a limitation imposed by others. As discussed previously, one factor that influences extrinsic motivation includes parents during childhood who utilized rewards or punishments in response to academic outcomes or as a means of discipline, or parents who remained uninvolved (Ginsburg and Bronstein, 1993; Gonzalez-DeHass, Willems and Holbein, 2005). Lisa's lack of involvement with Stefanie perhaps influenced her external motive orientation. Moreover, extrinsic motivation is also linked to authoritarian controlling parenting approaches, since we are aware of Lisa employing authoritarian means at times, it is important to note that this also plays an influential role, as children learn compliance/obedience which leads to rewards and lack of this leads to punishments (Grolnick and Slowiaczek, 1994). This inevitably leads to viewing tasks or goals in terms of rewards rather than enjoying the process. Moreover, individuals whose motivation is external and goal-oriented can over time internalize these motives, no longer requiring external influences. Instead, the internalized motive can become an integral component of a person's identity and sense of self (Hennessey et al., 2015). Scholars claim that these internalized motives become intrinsic because the individual has come to define the goals and/or limit themselves (Hennessey et al., 2015). The process of internalization involves a person gradually absorbing and assimilating previously externally governed behavior, making it a part of the self (Grolnick and Farkas, 2002). It is suggested that internalization is a natural process that children actively participate in as they take control of and master both their internal and external worlds (Grolnick and Farkas, 2002). More simply, extrinsic motivators across time become intrinsic, as continuous external goals are embedded in self-identity. One can view Stefanie through both forms of motivation based on this perspective. Furthermore, the collectivistic cultural view of intrinsic motivation is often linked to guidance by close friends or respected authorities, as well as preventative goals geared at preserving work or personal security (Hennessey et al., 2015). One can suggest that Stefanie's goal-oriented view of gaining money, knowledge or looking at the larger image, is a collectivistic perspective of maintaining security, safety and survival as a member of a close-knit cultural group. Such intrinsic motives in collectivist cultures are embedded in group ideals and values, often resembling extrinsic motivation as well, but are distinct (Hennessey et al., 2015).

Stefanie shares a memory that she feels has influenced who she is which is one rooted in her childhood. When she was between the ages of 6–12 years old, she remembers feeling anxious internally and worrying about what people thought of her. Our predictions of Lisa's daughter Stefanie having an insecure anxious attachment in the previous section could be a viable explanation now. As an adult, she observes herself still worrying and thinking similarly. She states that she is not sure what created this, but she has a hunch. She thinks that since her mother was quite "on top of things," indirectly making her feel like she "should" do something or be a specific way, perhaps, this made her feel more insecure or feel that she was not good enough. Growing up, she was not always aware of such insecurities, they went unnoticed, but recently, in these last 10 years, she has been observing and reflecting on what was happening inside her. As seen through literature by Ainsworth, Blehar, Waters and Wall (2015) and the 'Strange Situation,' when children perceive the attachment figure as unreliable, inconsistent and lacking stability, an anxious attachment is likely to occur. Moreover, children who are exposed to caregivers who are rejecting, angry and hold more restrictions, avoidant attachment may take place. Bowlby (1969) postulates that due to these early attachment experiences, the internal working model the child begins to store of themselves may be negative, similar to Stefanie forming core beliefs of herself not being good enough. One could suggest that her mother, Lisa's high demands, low responsiveness and forms of rejection through her authoritarian approach may have led Stefanie to feel that no matter what she does, it may never be enough, and that others may never find her enough based on her experience with her attachment figure. She has been coping with this by breaking her thoughts up into pieces, linking it to root causes and then using logical reasoning to rewrite this insecure narrative. She mentions that it does not always work since it is deeply rooted from childhood, but she is still trying. The distress Stefanie describes is similar to social anxiety as well. Knowingly, one of the most prevalent psychiatric issues affecting children of school age is anxiety (Wood et al., 2003). The causes and effects of childhood anxiety are complex and perplexing, despite the fact that it is a pervasive issue that impacts kids across childhood and adolescence (Wood et al., 2003). Parenting is a crucial factor that has been highlighted as a contributor to the emergence of childhood anxiety (Wood et al., 2003). Anxiety is an unpleasant sensation or feeling that is defined by a generalized threat of harm. On the other hand, social anxiety is characteristically defined as the dread of receiving negative judgments or evaluations by others, similar to Stefanie's description (Hofmann, Anu Asnaani and Hinton, 2010). Consequently, research has found that children who struggle with social anxiety often described their parents as being controlling, overly protective and inattentive (Rana, Akhtar and Tahir, 2013). Parental overcontrol is a pattern of controlling children's activities and routines excessively, making dictatorial decisions or demands on what to believe, think, feel and how to act (Wood et al., 2003). While authoritarian controlling parenting causes anxiety, maladjustment, and other behavioral issues in children, authoritative supportive parenting is favorably connected with emotional adjustment (Rana, Akhtar and Tahir, 2013). Adolescents who describe their parents as demanding, controlling, or unsupportive display increased psychological and behavioral problems, higher rates of anxiety disorders and internalizing issues in children (Rana, Akhtar and Tahir, 2013). It was also discovered that children's anxiety symptoms are caused by a lack of parental attachment which results in feelings of insecurity. Additionally, literature also suggests that social anxiety in children and adolescents is linked to the mothers' authoritarian and overprotective conduct (Rana, Akhtar and Tahir, 2013). Stefanie describes her mother as being "on top of things" which is assumed to be a controlling parenting approach or authoritarian with unrelenting expectations and demands on how to behave leading to an insecure attachment because if a child does not meet such standards, beliefs of being inadequate, unworthy, not good enough come to light (Bowlby, 1969). These beliefs are referred to as negative core beliefs with consequences such as low self-esteem, lack of self-worth, self-confidence, self-efficacy and self-identity which are often at the root of mental health struggles including Stefanie's social anxiety. This goes hand-in-hand with the Socio-Cultural Theory by Vygotsky which emphasizes the value of parenting interactions since a child learns a significant amount through social interaction with parents (Rana, Akhtar and Tahir, 2013). If Stefanie learned that it was tense and stressful when trying to meet demands her mother imposed, this stress may then be generalized around others, always trying to be a certain way around other individuals, leading to social anxiety. Therefore, it is understandable that one's opinion of their own self-image and self-worth can alter significantly during the course of the changes and difficulties experienced in this early relationship. Studies identified a negative correlation between tense parenting and depression, irritation, anxiety, and hostility (Rana, Akhtar and Tahir, 2013). Regarding gender differences, some investigations have revealed that female levels of social anxiety are higher than males. The emergence of social anxiety appears to be influenced by the relationship between gender socialization and the development of a child's response to stressors (Rana, Akhtar and Tahir, 2013).

Social norms and role expectations, which vary by culture, are closely related to social anxiety as well. Recognizing the complex relationship between social anxiety and culture, some research has concentrated on the psychopathological aspects of social anxiety globally (Hofmann, Anu Asnaani and Hinton, 2010). Strict social standards regarding what behavior is acceptable in particular social situations are meant to be provided in countries throughout Asia, South America, the Pacific Islands, and regions of Europe. Sanctions, such as removal from the group, are threatened against anyone who violates these social norms (Hofmann, Anu Asnaani and Hinton, 2010). It is crucial that people in these nations have their social behavior judged as suitable and beneficial. Additionally, in collectivistic but not individualistic societies, norms are powerful determinants of life contentment (Hofmann, Anu Asnaani and Hinton, 2010). Therefore, it is probable that social anxiety and other emotional issues are caused by a mismatch between a person's cultural orientation and cultural norms, especially if that person exhibits an extreme allocentric orientation or strong idiocentric values (Hofmann, Anu Asnaani and Hinton, 2010). Compared to individualistic nations, collective nations revealed higher numbers in social anxiety and panic. It's likely that social norms and standards for openly showing experiences of social anxiety are related to variances in reported degrees of social anxiety among cultures (Hofmann, Anu Asnaani and Hinton, 2010). According to research, independence and interdependence are inversely connected with embarrassability and the fear of being judged adversely, both of which are significant components of the symptomatic presentation of social anxiety (Hofmann, Anu Asnaani and Hinton, 2010). Consequently, being raised in a collectivistic culture could have also played a key role in Stefanie's social anxiety development as well.

To the question "what do parents of successful children have in common?," Stefanie responded with, "there must be a link there." She says that every child and person is unique and not everything works for everyone. She believes that open communication such as speaking to children openly/honestly, explaining difficult concepts or why certain rules or actions of discipline were taken (e.g., "I love you, but I am doing this because . . . "), establishing boundaries that incorporate closeness and healthy limits are key to successful children. Stefanie demonstrates strong characteristics of authoritative parenting as well as supportive parenting, as according to Kotaman (2013) and Baumrind (1996, 2005). Authoritative parents respect their children's sense of self and recognize them as distinct persons, they clearly define boundaries and direct children toward developmental challenges and they substitute reasoning, rationalization, explanation, monitoring, and modelling for punitive disciplinary techniques. As mentioned previously, according to Cohen & Mannarino (2008), when emotionally neglectful or distressing parenting experiences are present during childhood, it is likely that children may exhibit oppositional behaviors since the traumatic experience they endured as children was perceived as unjust and incorrect. We use this as a means to understand the change in the parenting approaches Stefanie has compared to her mother. She explains, after a certain age, when children are older, parents imposing forceful rules or disciplinary measures are not effective, therefore, communicating and explaining why something is useful or not, is more beneficial. She also believes that repetition is very important as well. She explains, "even if you speak to your child and feel that they are not listening to you because you repeat the same things over again, your child may normally respond by saying 'stop telling me the same things again'." Despite that, she has observed overtime that her daughter has retained some of the information through her repetition and claims "certain topics are registered in their mind and it helps them later." As is commonly known, repetition is a vital aspect of learning and retaining concepts and repetition priming has been linked to storing information in implicit memory. More specifically, a child can build an understanding and even try to replicate when words, ideas, or skills are repeated to them. She believes that parents who support their children emotionally, verbally, physically, in all ways that they can, help in raising successful children. Stefanie's last statement once again follows Baumrind's (1967, 1996, 2005) description of authoritative parents, where security or responsiveness and direction across several domains are provided to children in order for them to engage in experiences that will mold them and help them reach their full potential. Authoritative parents step in when necessary but they don't take over their children's responsibilities (Baumrind, 1971). These parents are responsive, loving, affectionate and caring. Additionally, these traits reflect psychological health and high self-esteem in children (Kotaman, 2013). By incorporating all these aspects of authoritative supportive parenting, Stefanie also models self-regulation practices, communication skills, critical thinking, problem-solving abilities, emotional validation and positive beliefs of oneself, safety, acceptance, secure attachments, empathy, and pro-social skills for her daughter.

Lastly, she discusses aspects of how her mother raised her that she either did not like or it just did not work for her and she consciously tried not to repeat this pattern when raising her daughter. She expresses that, at times, she was not very successful in avoiding generational patterns because it is embedded deep inside her, coming out unconsciously like a habit. For example, she shares that her mother (Lisa) was very authoritarian using physical means of discipline (e.g., use of belt or slipper) especially when Stefanie used to respond back in arguments with disagreement. Stefanie has never done this with her daughter who is now 21 years old. One can view Stefanie's experiences of control and physical abuse as traumatic and an adverse childhood experience (Felitti et al., 1998; Cohen and Mannarino, 2008; Jaberghaderi et al., 2004; Osofsky, 2018). There are countless psychological consequences to such forms of discipline and abuse including: Post-Traumatic Stress Disorder (PTSD), increased depressive and anxiety symptoms, impulsive or risky behaviors, suicidal tendencies, and behavioral disorders (Cohen & Mannarino, 2008; Jaberghaderi et al., 2004). Moreover, physical abuse by parental figures is associated to insecure attachments, as parents are the cause of fear, abuse, uncertainty and distress in the child, leading to them being emotionally dysregulated, vulnerable, lonely, angry, hypervigilant, with an overactive fight/flight/freeze—threat system and helpless (Howe and Fearnley; 1999). Stefanie further asserts that physical punishment would follow when she voiced her viewpoints during arguments or conflicts as a result of her disagreeing or disobeying her mother (Kotaman, 2013). This has a direct connection to authoritarian control, where parents establish beliefs, standards, and guidelines, and children are expected to adhere to them (Baumrind, 1996). This leaves little room for children to try to build their own perspectives, explore their ideas or gain a meaningful understanding from the parent. A rigid approach to parenting prevents children from learning critical and flexible thinking, curiosity, problem-solving techniques, communication skills, self-esteem, or developing a sense of self (Kotaman, 2013). She affirms that she does not agree with physical punishment and she believes that there are other ways to discipline or teach a child. As with all of our stories, we notice again how previous generations' use of corporal discipline is something children choose to avoid with their young nowadays, either because it was a painful experience they do not wish to recreate the trauma or because it was not useful. Again, as Elliman and Lynch (2000) similarly claim, corporal punishment only leads to mild short-term compliance in children but does not increase long-term understanding or behavior change. In fact, the negative consequences such as long-term antisocial behavior, anxiety, depression, low self-esteem, substance use as well as significant reductions in positive outcomes such as moral reflection, learning, awareness, and empathy, outweigh any positive or effective influence (Elliman and Lynch, 2000).

However, Stefanie did maintain certain aspects of how she was raised when raising her daughter. For instance, she was always quite close to her mother and her daughter is the same with her as well. Additionally, when she was growing up, her mother was engaged in her social life like asking to meet her friends, spending time with them and getting to know everyone and Stefanie has replicated this with her daughter and her social circle as well. Parental involvement in several different manners, is a form of supportive parenting through engagement, responsiveness, social as well as emotional validation (Kuppens and Ceulemans, 2019). Lisa's involvement in certain aspects of Stefanie's life allowed for some emotional connection and attachment to form, aiding with or serving as a buffer against the psychological distance felt due to authoritarian control experienced frequently. It is understandable that these moments of connection and warmth is a positive aspect of parenting that Stefanie wanted to maintain. She also mentions that when she was growing up, she had a more traditional upbringing with her father around often but for her daughter, because she is divorced, she raised her alone in a single parent household. Lastly, she also shares that her daughter reminds her of her mother in many ways, which makes her happy, because her daughter is strong and resilient, similar to her mother, Lisa. She says her mother is her rock. It is interesting to observe that despite having a distressing childhood experience with control and punitive measures, Stefanie has formed a secure and close relationship with her mother till date. One could assume that this may be linked to some security in attachment, while on the other hand, closeness could also be connected to cultural norms of families as groups maintaining harmony or that Stefanie has gone through her inner psychological healing to work through difficult thoughts, beliefs and emotions to maintain a strong bond.

Story 6: Stefanie (Parental Role)

Stefanie begins her parental role interview by relaying the inspiration behind her parenting approach. She described that quite a lot of her inspiration was mentioned above in her interview as a daughter, but an additional aspect she consciously implemented when raising her own child was physical affection. She shares that she does not remember her mother hugging her growing up, perhaps, she did hug her when she was very young, but she cannot actively recall it. Stefanie links this to her mother's family of origin, saying that her grandfather was not very physically affectionate and her grandmother, despite being very sweet as a person, was not physically affectionate either. She suggests that perhaps, this is why her mother never hugged her and she always had this in mind when raising her daughter. Feeling loved (emotionally and behaviorally) is vital for a child's optimal and healthy growth/development

(Sabey et al., 2018). The literature on child development affirms the value of touch, physical tenderness and happy feelings in a parents' relationships with children (Hyson, Whitehead and Prudhoe, 1988). According to prenatal studies, the sense of touch is the first to develop in the human embryo. The healthy functions of a young child is directly influenced by the emotive nature of early parental behavior, including but not limited to physical affection. The development of a children's positive self-concepts and prosocial behavior has distinctly been connected—in the child-rearing literature—to adults' provision of warmth and nurturing (Hyson, Whitehead and Prudhoe, 1988). In a parent-child interaction, children typically get their earliest experiences of feeling loved and understanding the concept of love, and those who have more loving parents benefit in a variety of ways, ranging from more peer competency in childhood to fewer mental health adjustment issues later in life (for instance, drug abuse and depression) (Sabey et al., 2018). It's important to comprehend how parents show their love to their children through behavior since specific parenting techniques require the parent to develop a strong bond and attachment with their child throughout time (Sabey et al., 2018).

A body of studies have demonstrated that emotionally unresponsive maternal behavior affects the child's positive emotional expressions significantly, particularly when the adult's unresponsiveness contrasts with previously good interactions (Hyson, Whitehead and Prudhoe, 1988). As we know, this inconsistency of parental behaviors leads to an insecure or anxious attachment, as the child is unable to predict or understand the parent, earning the child an abundance of overwhelming emotions. The development of secure bonds, which appear to result from the caregiver's emotional and physical responsiveness to the child, supports the ability of the child to explore and be curious with an internal sense of stability as well as a sense of self. Similarly, according to the Attachment Theory, this loving relationship grows as parents exhibit sensitive and responsive behaviors that increase their child's sense of safety and security (Bowlby, 1969; Ainsworth, 1979; Sabey et al., 2018). In other words, children will form a solid attachment to their parents to the extent that parents are "attuned" to their children's emotional and physical needs (Sabey et al., 2018). These themes are in line with the Attachment Theory, which contends that parental love takes on particular manifestations, such as the provision of structure, support and comfort during instances where the child is distressed, and during positive interactions or experiences together (e.g., playing or doing activities together) (Bowlby, 1969; Ainsworth, 1979; Ainsworth et al., 2015). Children prefer to have close physical contact with caregivers, according to studies on attachment (Hyson, Whitehead and Prudhoe, 1988). Therefore, it is important to emphasize that the presence of positive interactions is just as important as the absence of negative interactions in determining the quality of a parent-child relationship.

Studies have demonstrated the importance of positive touch (i.e., hugging, kissing, embracing) for children's growth and wellbeing in particular (Sabey et al., 2018). Touch, thus seems to be a significant action via which parental love is expressed and felt among the families in this study, supporting the ground-breaking work by Harry Harlow in 1958 on Contact Comfort (Sabey et al., 2018). It is understandable that Stefanie's deprivation of physical love or touch from her mother made this a focal point in the child-rearing of her daughter, which once more supports Stefanie's use of a holistically supportive parenting approach, including her expressions of love. Stefanie shares that she used to hug her daughter a lot when she was a child and they continue to be affectionate with each other till this day. Stefanie's continued expression of love to her now adult-daughter may play a role in maintaining a secure attachment and a quality relationship. Stefanie also wanted to instill certain values in her daughter such as being a good person; this links to a story she shares towards the end of her interview where such values were observed in her daughter.

To the question "what was helpful and what did you avoid as a parent?," Stefanie responded that she learned to avoid controlling or trying to over-guide or overprotect her daughter from making mistakes. She explains that, until her daughter was a teenager, she was quite a pleasant, easy and a calm child to raise. However, when her daughter turned 18, she began changing and exploring new aspects of herself. She started to go out more and return home at later hours and she had even gotten a job at a café/bar without consulting Stefanie—due to which she would return home at 5 in the morning. Stefanie felt like these changes happened quite suddenly and initially, it was quite shocking and she began worrying about her daughter making wrong decisions. At the start, Stefanie continued her usual parenting routine (i.e., calling her daughter to check on her, advising her not to do certain things and what would be more useful). But she realized, this was not working anymore like it used to and they began quarreling more. Stefanie understood that something needed to change and she decided to try a different way and started using logic in order to reduce the disputes between them, move forward and better this new version of their relationship. She decided to let go of trying to guide her daughter and observe how her daughter manages her life—this being 2 years ago. Since then, their relationship has grown significantly and has become much better. Her daughter chose to leave her job at the café/bar herself because she realized that it was not for her. Literature has termed the age range between 18 and 25 years as "emerging adulthood," or in other words, a time when young people are still experimenting with different life choices, evading full adult duties, and tackling various relational and personal obligations (Kloep and Hendry, 2010). Studies have emphasized the multiple elements of adult growth, including the numerous changes that young adults encounter in the areas of work, home, and health and how these distinct experiences relate to one another. These influential transitions can be linked to the Ecological Theory of Bronfenbrenner and Morris that suggests that the family functions as a microsystem inside a larger social scale (the macro system) with both interacting and influencing the other (Kloep and Hendry, 2010). During such a transition, parents are tasked with providing both financial and emotional support for their children (Kloep and Hendry, 2010). Researchers have observed that the longest era of parenthood—during which children reach adolescent and young adulthood but parents are still in their prime—is poorly understood, as are the many aspects that affect it, such as the rewards and costs of parenting (Kloep and Hendry, 2010). During this stage of emerging adulthood, parents begin altering their positions into friend roles with a trend toward permissive parenting (Kloep and Hendry, 2010). According to a few researchers, parenting styles that begin promoting autotomy facilitate a child's maturing and individuation during these early adult years (Kloep and Hendry, 2010). However, research by Kloep and Hendry (2010) found that parents allowing their adult offspring to pursue and attain mature independence seemed to present some challenges for the majority of parents. Although Kloep and Hendry (2010) specifically examined parental perspectives on emerging adults leaving home, a substantial amount of their findings can be used in understanding parental attitudes towards letting go of some level of control towards their young adult children and the consequences of the opposite. It is suggested that some parents struggle to accept their children's desire for independence while others use a variety of tactics—whether deliberately or unconsciously—to put off "letting go" (Kloep and Hendry, 2010). The inability of parents to "let go" was expressively related to whether or not they saw their children as mature individuals (Kloep and Hendry, 2010). This willingness depended on whether parents approved of their children's lifestyle choice: with agreement, parents could celebrate their children's autonomous triumphs, limit their intervention and grant them adult status (Kloep and Hendry, 2010). However, any attempt at independence that conflicted with parental perspective was frequently regarded with anger and viewed as a signal of immaturity (Kloep and Hendry, 2010). Additionally, the ability to "let go" often seems to reflect a parent's desire to preserve their parental position for as long as possible rather than a young person's own behavior (Kloep and Hendry, 2010). Moreover, overindulgence of young adults appears to have a negative impact on their acquisition of many adult skills. According to research, overprotective parenting results in early adulthood dependency and diminished autonomy (Kloep and Hendry, 2010). Dependency increases the likelihood of maladjustment and mental health issues like depression, substance abuse and codependency challenges later in life (Kloep and Hendry, 2010). Thus, it appears that a parents unwillingness to let their children reach adulthood may contribute in some way to the development of "emerging adults" who are hesitant to assume adult duties (Kloep and Hendry, 2010). Independent emerging adults are more likely to form mature adult-to-adult interactions and have reported having better relationships with their parents (Kloep and Hendry, 2010). With regards to Stefanie, the above research supports her reluctance to let go of her previous authoritative parenting practices into a more permissive style enabling space for her daughter's autonomy. Kloep and Hendry's (2010) research also supports Stefanie's unwillingness to perceive her daughter as mature and independent which was related to her daughters choices, such as working at a bar till late hours, which was not something Stefanie approved of, causing her to believe this was perhaps immature or not sound thinking on her daughters part. Consequently, this was causing turmoil in her parent-child relationship coinciding with past studies. As research has suggested, overcontrol in such stages of life has negative effects on adult development of independence while promoting autonomy with a permissive supportive stance allows for young adults to learn adult responsibilities and better parent-child relationships. We see this represented with Stefanie and her daughter as well, signifying the importance of parental adaptability, permissiveness in later parenting behaviors and releasing their children into the macrosystem of society to grow and develop into mature individuals. Likewise, Stefanie says, she grasped that her daughter needed to have her own experiences, to learn for herself and make her own mistakes like everyone does since this is the best way we learn. Stefanie also mentions how she used this philosophy to navigate other changes with her daughter, for instance, when she had exams at college, she would go out with friends instead of studying. This was not how Stefanie approached college life herself and she tried to guide her daughter to follow the same path she did. When Stefanie was in college, she would wake up at 9AM, eat breakfast, study for about 4 hours, take a break to have lunch, rest/go out/watch tv, study again for 4–5 hours in the evening and go to bed. But, when she tried to advise her daughter on this, her daughter responded, "that is how you did it, I will do it my way." Stefanie chose to then let her daughter find her own path, to which her daughter demonstrated positive results, with good grades in all classes. Her daughter still goes out and returns home at later hours, but Stefanie is more relaxed about this now as she now observes that her daughter is mature, healthy, safe, happy and makes sound decisions. She has come to terms that her daughter does things differently. As parents, we have lived a whole life prior to our children's arrival and we want to use our experiences to help guide them so that they don't make the mistakes we once did. This is a natural response but it is not always useful because it leaves no room for children to learn through their own experience. This is a struggle in parenting, letting go at the appropriate life stage and allowing children to grow into adults because parents often always see them as children.

When it comes to motivation, Stefanie discusses a story of how she tried to motivate her daughter to continue a hobby she was very passionate about which was dancing. She explained, her daughter stopped classes as she was not satisfied with the dance school anymore. She had been going to this school since she was 4 years old, but recently, she felt left behind in larger classes and was not receiving enough attention to grow her skill. Stefanie was very supportive when her daughter stopped dancing, discussing together if she perhaps wanted to try out other activities, trying to understand if there was something else bothering her and processing with her the emotions she feels by discontinuing a big part of her life. In order to keep her daughter motivated to seek out a hobby again, Stefanie would search for opportunities available and present them to her daughter as options she had and remind her that if she wanted to go back to dancing, she would support her. Eventually, her daughter found a dance school she liked and will begin attending it in a few months. Stefanie also acknowledged that perhaps her daughter also needed a break from her previous activities to try something new and accepted that she would eventually return to doing things she likes. As we know from previous interviews discussing motivation, extrinsic motivation is participating in a task or activity to meet an external demand or to obtain a reward while intrinsic motivation is participating in a task or activity based on pleasure and contentment from the process (Turner, Chandler and Heffer, 2009). We can observe a theme of intrinsic drive established in Stefanie's daughter as she enjoys the process of dancing. Stefanie contributes to internal motivation by being encouraging, processing thoughts and emotions with her daughter, and discovering other enjoyable activities with her. In this scenario, an indirect external goal is being achieved, namely, her daughter's skill in dancing will grow. However, her daughter's participation in dancing was not about the goal, but rather, the process and experience. She stated that her daughter has been dancing since she was a child and that she enjoys the act of it. Furthermore, research shows that autonomy-supportive home situations boosts intrinsic autonomous motivation (Turner, Chandler and Heffer, 2009). Stefanie provides a supportive environment for her daughter, including when she decides to drop out of classes, exploring her pursuit of other opportunities, and recognizes that her daughter may simply require a pause from activities. Her continuous involvement, commitment, acknowledgement, warmth and responsiveness to emotional, physical and external struggles her daughter experiences supports Baumrind's (1971) authoritative parenting . It also supports Kuppens and Ceulemans' (2019) portrayal of supportive parenting. Similarly, children with authoritative parents, such as Stefanie, were more motivated, capable and purpose driven than children with permissive or controlling parents (Turner, Chandler and Heffer, 2009). According to research, authoritative parenting styles in a parent-child connection promotes a child's sense of mastery (i.e., belief in managing one's circumstances), as well as internal motivation, self-confidence, self-esteem, and self-efficacy (Turner, Chandler and Heffer, 2009). We observe this with Stefanie's daughter who chose to continue dancing in the future and sought out another dance school emphasizing her internal adoration of the experience.

Stefanie upheld values of organization and honesty with her daughter which she says was unconsciously similar to how she was raised. But mostly, she tried to model to her daughter appropriate behaviors. She believes that, if your child sees how you are and how you operate, they are more likely to mimic aspects of this. She never explicitly told her daughter "not to lie, not to steal, not to harm, be kind," she aimed at being a visual example of these values and embodied it. Based on the Social Learning Theory, modeling goes back to how children learn about the world. Children tend to mimic and learn through observation of their parents' specific behaviors such as genuine effort and altruistic attitudes towards others (Sharma, 2021; Marti-Vilar, Serrano-Pastor and Sala, 2019). Stefanie's approach also reflects Baumrind's (1971) authoritative approach that discusses modeling or demonstrating empathy, prosocial attitudes, regulation and coping with distress. This also coincides with Kotaman (2013) and Kuppens and Ceulemans (2019) reporting that authoritative parenting employs modeling, reasoning and explaining to foster healthy development and socialization in children. Furthermore, attachment literature claims that children who are securely attached to their parents are more likely to be prosocial because a sense of security is established when parents are not only responsive and sensitive, but also supportive of their children's explorations (Ainsworth, 1979; Sutton, 2019; Wong, Konishi and Kong, 2021). According to these studies, it can be suggested that through Stefanie's supportive parenting approach with warmth (emotion and physical), modeling, guidance and responsiveness as well as healthy boundaries, she has formed a secure attachment with her daughter, allowing for prosocial and helping behaviors. This is also evident in the next paragraph as we observe her daughter choosing a helping profession and displaying altruistic, nurturing and empathic attitudes. Lastly, higher helping and empathic prosocial actions are positively connected with collectivism and individuals from collectivistic worlds, according to Marti-Vilar, Serrano-Pastor and Sala (2019). In collectivistic societies, interconnectedness and social (e.g., family) obligations are prized in order to sustain societal and group harmony (Wong, Konishi and Kong, 2021). Since Stefanie resides in Greece where collectivism is prominent, cultural norms also play a key role in modeling and molding children to certain societal values as well.

Finally, Stefanie shares a memory where she felt she was a successful parent. Recently, Stefanie's grandfather had a scheduled surgery at the hospital and Stefanie was delighted to observe that her daughter had solely accompanied her grandfather for four days and nights to take care of him. Stefanie anticipated that her daughter, who is presently pursuing a career as a nurse, would stay throughout the day and return home at night. Instead, her daughter offered to take on the responsibility to care for her grandfather alone. Stefanie expresses her appreciation for her daughter's desire to help people and knowing that her child will be there for others in crucial life events makes her feel successful. Additionally, she feels successful observing her daughter become a strong, loving and sensitive woman. In another recent incident, Stefanie had just had her COVID-19 immunization and wasn't feeling well. At the time, her daughter was away but she returned home to tend to Stefanie and expressed love and support through physical touch (i.e., hugging, cuddling and kissing). She is content that her daughter is a good person, who is kind and is able to express appropriate affection. Given that Stefanie expressed physical affection and love frequently towards her daughter, we also observe this effectively mirrored in her daughter as well. Stefanie's warmness, affection and support as a parent has played an important role in her daughter's life, displaying traits of gentleness, compassion, responsiveness, altruism and prosocial behaviors towards others.

Stefanie's daughter was unavailable for an interview.

Chapter 5

Stories From the Middle East

Before proceeding with the following cultural narratives, it is useful to emphasize that the interviewer and researcher of this particular section is seen as an expert who was born and raised in the Middle East (Kuwait). The participants from different parts of the Middle East living in Kuwait were chosen based on voluntary participation in sharing their subjective impressions of parenting and childhood.

STORY 1: NADIA, RYAN, LU & ALI

Different parenting styles result in different outcomes in the children and their decisions within life. Therefore, parenting styles affect every aspect of a child's life. The parenting style can affect how the child behaves, their ability to make decisions, and the child's health and general development. A healthy parenting style includes the parent providing support and frequent interactions with their child to build a strong bond and trust between the child and the parent. Nadia used a different parenting approach by participating in activities with her children to acknowledge their needs and offering support where necessary. The use of this different style of parenting stems from the cultural and social relationship between mother and child. Nadia's goal within motherhood was to raise children who can maintain a healthy social life and a mentally stable lifestyle. Nadia also emphasized on providing her children with access to good education to allow them to succeed throughout their lives. Research shows that past relationships between parent and child affect the growth of the child's development, when faced with their own relationships as they grow up and progress into adulthood; and hence styles of parenting change as well as goals when they become a parent. These goals she set while raising her children played a major role in her parenting style and interactions towards her children. Her approach includes providing mentorship for her children and giving them the space to pursue what they truly strive for in life. Nadia also aimed to raise children who are successful. The goal is to provide a supportive environment for her children to be successful within their own careers and social conditions. She additionally supported them as she was an attentive listener. Nadia was also aware of her children's abilities when supporting their development within their social and educational enviroments. Using these tools of support, she was able to guide them when necessary and provide the help needed to overcome the challenges life presented along the way. She also challenged her three children to develop more intelligent and analytical skills by encouraging them to think deeply and be further aware of their purpose within life. Having a purpose in life is critical as it inspires someone to be more dedicated, energetic and resilient; psychologists believe that a purpose is a long-term motivator that drives people to sucess, and helps people drive a more steady and stable relationship (Albanese, Geller and Russo, 2019). As a result of Nadia's actions, all her children succeeded within life and their careers: Ryan being a businessman, Lu being a doctor and Ali a soon-to-be politician. These children are not just successful career-wise; they also have expressed social success as they have maintained admirable personalities. They demonstrated positive traits that include being caring, ambitious and social. They also performed selfless actions towards other individuals. Nadia's parenting style has provided them with the chance to achieve this success. One of the vital tools in her parenting approach was that Nadia chose to incorporate encouragement of independence within her children's behaviors and lifestyles. She encouraged them to be independent within every aspect of their lives. Therefore, she accepted them for who they are and supported them in achieving their dreams and aspirations. She also acknowledges that her children are unique within their life approach. Consequently, she supports her children by guiding them to achieve what they are most passionate about. Undeniably, mothers act and represent the pillar of a family. Mothers are expected to offer love, guidance, and support in a non-judgmental manner towards children. No matter how old a child gets, they will always turn back to their mother for their guidance and assurance. Psychologists urge parents not to seize but to inspire and assist their children since they are the best teachers in their child's life, therefore, maintaining a good parent-child relationship is essential. Case studies show that relationships are an essential criteria in the development of a positive and empowering connection between parent and child since parents are children's first teachers, parents play a crucial role in the development of the child (Albanese, Geller and Russo, 2019). There is further emphasis that knowing your child, including his/her capabilities and weaknesses, would help parents to guide and encourage their children to do better within life.

A child's learning and socialization process is influenced by the parents parenting style. Parents who raise happy children are more involved in their child's life since a child's development lies at the root of their parents. Nadia used an authoritative parenting style while raising her children. The authoritative parenting style includes the establishment of clear rules and specific boundaries for the children. Authoritative parenting is different from authoritarian parents as she explained the logical reasoning behind applying rules and restrictions for her children. Authoritative parents also show warmth; even though they set high standards and expect their children to adopt a certain behavior, they are also empathetic (Muller & Kerbow, 2018). Nadia also engaged in further communication with her children. As a concerned parent, she was ready to listen to her children's opinions and concerns regarding different topics. The approach of explaining the logical reasoning of rules and restrictions enabled her children to become independent thinkers who recognize their purpose in life (Albanese, Geller and Russo, 2019). Within the parenting style of authoritative parenting, it is vital to establish open communication and the explanation of rules. Being an authoritative parent, she often had discussions with her children to clearly understand and establish their needs. Besides discussions, she also tries to focus on positive reinforcement. Additionally, Nadia set specific expectations within her children's lives. She also encouraged her children to exhibit self-regulated behavior; She gave her children the space and the freedom to think and work through life challenges and overall, her role was to advise and provide guidance. Like other authoritative parents, she showed warmth and understanding, but set high standards and expected her three children to adopt disciplined behavior that includes positive traits such as selflessness.

Since mothers are the most influential figures in a child's life, Nadia proved this by helping her children recognize their weaknesses and encouraging them to utilize their abilities. When conversing with her children, she inspired them to pursue what they are most passionate about in life without being distracted by other things. She pushed them to follow their dreams by encouraging them throughout their lives and enrolling them into the best schools. Psychologists point out that there are several factors that can predict a child's success and these include the type of parenting style used to raise a child: spending time with a child, letting the child make his/her own decisions, and maintaining good parent-child relations are all important factors that inspire a child to succeed (Muller & Kerbow, 2018). Psychologists warn parents to not to be strict because when a parent provides instruction rather than direction to children, children may lack the ability to figure out how to solve problems on their own, while on the other hand, providing them with the freedom and instructions when needed is more beneficial to the child in the long run (Muller & Kerbow, 2018). According to Albanese, Geller and Russo (2019), the direct involvement of parents in guiding their children affects the child's ability to be in control of their life. Parents need to be sensitive and caring while at the same time provide the necessary opportunities and give space to the child in order for the child to become a fully independent thinker.

For Ryan, Lu, and Ali to succeed in different careers returns back to the way in which Nadia was aware of her children's strengths and weaknesses. She inspired them to succeed by pushing them in a specific direction that was in line with their different abilities. Therefore, in this situation, we can observe that investing in the early parent-child relationship and implementing communication results in good outcomes towards the children and their behavior. Having a successful early parent-child relationship including not being controlling and instead nurturing children by using methods like positive mannerisms and warmth is more effective. The methods of positivity would result in the children's happiness, success and satisfaction later on in their life. In contrast, when the opposite approach is used, including the children experiencing controlling parents who choose their careers for them and use physical punishments as disciplinary lessons on the children; children will not have the opportunity to explore and be aware of their abilities and consequently, this will impact their lifestyle. They will always rely on their parents to give them direction within life and its challenges. As a result, they will find it difficult to deal with life's challenges as adults since they lack the skills to cope. This will eventually lead to depression, anxiety, other psychological conditions and low self-esteem.This type of trauma on children undergoing such a lifestyle and responsibilities creates traumatic experiences in the future, possibly preventing any stable relationships and a chance to live a life without having complications (Putnam, 2006).

STORY 2: YOUSIF

Yousif is perplexed when another parent provides a child with an opportunity and it makes him think about taking different parenting approaches than his own parents did with him. His parents did not give him space to grow as a child and did not allow him to dream like a normal kid. His parents were obsessed with achieving their dreams through Yousif, which affected his childhood and these different approaches to parenting could have a different effect on children. Strict parenting was applied in this story because his parents were always strict about what he should do, and most of the time, he remained indoors despite having friends who he could have interacted with in alternative circumstances. An authoritarian parenting style does not involves closeness between a parent and a child and would be low in flexibility and this type of parenting could put pressure on children whereby they could feel the burden of performing based on the needs of the parents (Fraser, McIntyre and Manby, 2022). This can be seen as a form of neglect. Studies have shown the brain regions in neglected children displaying signs of underdevelopment in emotional control. Early childhood neglect, particularly prenatal neglect, has an impact on the size and functionality of the developing brain, while also creating academic challenges due to the pressure of performing well in school (Avdibegovi and Brki, 2020).

His story made us think of what children who have undergone different parenting styles express after growing up, and in Yousif's case, he reenacted his parent's dreams instead of his own. He was not able to live a necessary childhood as he was constantly pressured to perform better for his parents, a factor that would affect a child drastically. Strict parenting mainly revolves around unquestionable obedience, whereby the child is not allowed to question anything concerning the decisions made by their parents and since this parenting style mainly concentrates on discipline; the child is expected to be what their parents want them to be against all odds involved in life (Bornstein, 2012). Parents are under constant pressure to see their children succeed in the dreams they have set for them despite not having achieved those dreams themselves. These parents want to see their children as successful people in the community so that it would bring pride to their name. This links back to our discussion of a collective culture and how every individual is expected to pursue a career that will reflect positively on their group or parents in this case. In most cases, there is no choice for the child when it comes to decision-making compared to what the parents would achieve by enforcing their own dreams on their children.

Yousif, in this case, was extremely drained and detested the life in which he grew up knowing. This demonstrates a form of emotional neglect through actions or inactions by the caregiver that may result in the child developing behavioral, affective, or mental disorders (Hildyard and Wolfe, 2002). Due to such experiences, Yousif expressed wanting to raise his children differently and explained that he would rather provide them with more options to choose from while discovering what interests them rather than having them work towards what he has set for them to do in school. For example, he expressed that he was interested in a course involving history and literature compared to the engineering profession he got for his parents. Authoritarian parents do not nurture children but ensure that they can control them by making viable decisions for them (Bornstein, 2012). Despite the life belonging to the child, children are not allowed to choose what they should do or learn. The child's academic life over the years will appear to be a traumatic event for them as growing up under authoritarian types of parenting will undeniably lead to feelings of pressure resulting from the need to perform based on the needs of their parents (LaCapra, 2016). The learning process in this situation becomes an issue that can cause stress to children, mainly if they cannot perform based on the parent's demands.

The approach also involves corporal punishment when the child does not perform as required in the family setting. Authoritarian parents concentrate on their children's failures compared to their achievements. The children are mainly required to achieve every set target by the parents despite having different interests in life (Kuppens & Ceulemans, 2019). A child's life is significantly affected by what the parents think they should achieve or what society has set to be a successful person. The parents, in this case, expect no mistakes from their children, and they are expected to not bend any rules within the family or any aspects that have been put in place. The children raised within set rules can grow to understand the need to follow directions, but would also be unsatisfied with the lives they have achieved for themselves within the living aspects (Deblinger et al., 2011). Yousif is not satisfied with the career his parents chose for him and is always finding ways in which he could see better meaning in his life. In some cases, society has modeled individuals into thinking there is unquestionable success through most famous careers.

The authoritarian parenting style could be psychologically draining for children and especially when they believe they are not good enough. Parenting can be a significant cause of a child's trauma based on what they have been exposed to at a young age. Strict parents do not consider their children's psychological aspects which puts them at risk of traumatic events throughout their lives. Corporal punishments have been used over the years and could lead to trauma in children when they remember how badly they were physically abused or even injured in their own homes. In Yousif's case, he was more emotionally abused rather than physically. The mental wellness of children can be ignored, but it affects the development process of children and their adulthood (Cohen & Mannarino, 2008). Within certain aspects of life, Yousif seems to be stressed by events of his childhood rather than the current adulthood issues. The events he witnessed in his own home might cause insecurities, especially in his career, and he could question if he is good enough to continue in the same job for the rest of his life. Toxic stress has been linked to what children in strict homes have experienced leading to mental and physical health problems.

Research studies confirm that most parents still believe that having strict rules produce better-behaved children. However, this is not the case. The authoritarian parenting style negatively impacts children since parents fail to address their children's mental health. As a result, children raised in a strict environment, like Yousif was, are likely to develop low self-esteem (Garcia et al., 2020). According to Chen et al. (2019), children learn by modeling, meaning if children have authoritarian parents, they will likely be authoritarian in the future. This is because authoritarian parents fail to acknowledge their children's weaknesses. Instead, they make it clear that some parts of their children's traits are not acceptable. Therefore, these children often struggle to manage and cope with some of their feelings (Garcia et al., 2020). Hence, they feel afraid to try and work through the weaknesses they possess, which leads to anger or depression. Strict parenting is unhealthy because children are taught that parents are always right and all they learn is to obey without asking any questions. However, this affects them later in life when they fail to question those in authority when needed. Additionally, these children are not well prepared to take responsibility since they only tend to follow orders (Garcia et al., 2020).

Discipline and corporal punishments are some of the old approaches to parenting which have mostly been abandoned, however, as some authoritarian parents are still present, we would like to stress upon the fact that harsh discipline makes children more rebellious when growing up. This explains why Yousif now prefers to raise his children differently by giving them the freedom to choose what they are interested in doing rather than giving them direction on what to do since he grew up in a society where he noticed the different parenting styles and outcomes (Chen et al., 2019). Based on his personal experience Yousif would rather let his children choose the subjects that they feel comfortable with than force them and mold them into something they are not.

Being authoritarian limits children's ability to explore and discover their abilities, and the worst aspect of this style of parenting is that they undermine the parent-child relationship. Such parents fail to show the empathy needed for their children to feel safe and accepted (Chen et al., 2019). The child and parent relationship experiences difficulties as children lose interest in reaching out to their parents for advice or affirmation. Children who are parented in a strict environment are likely to fight with their parents to attain their freedom (Chen et al., 2019). The ideal environment that can nurture children to adopt acceptable behavior is where children feel accepted despite their flaws. Children need to be given room to explore on their own to become independent thinkers in the future. Confinement to this extent of control not only suppresses a lot of creativity but can lead to toxic thought processes and eventually seep into society. When individuals experience such levels of control, they try to find an alternative way of parenting their own children; however, their authoritarian style resurfaces itself, creating a disruptive relationship with their children. We can also relate the theory of attachment to this; as the child's confidence in the extension of themselves through the caregivers behavior and readiness is a solid base to which they can freely explore new places that are safe while receiving support or even having a "comfort zone" by being close to the attached figure (Bowlby, 1969). For a developing child, exploring and discovering a new environment is important to enable them to build higher self-confidence in which results in independence.

STORY 3: LEYLA

Leyla starts her story by relaying on how she is a single parent who "fails" to have a partner. She graduated in 2011 with a degree in family medicine and began working immediately after receiving her degree. She credits much of her sense of accomplishment to the fact that she married young. Even though she was caring for her son at the time, she expresses being really grateful that she had the chance to acquire her degree. She was able to effectively rehabilitate herself, graduate from college and obtain employment despite the failure of her marriage. She regards it as a great honor that others view her as someone from whom they can obtain knowledge. She began by reflecting on her own upbringing, observing that her parents were "realistic" in the way that they frequently worried over her grades and career. She expressed that there was nothing wrong with this since most parents want the best for their children. However, she believed that it was impossible for her to build an emotional connection with her parents or gain their attention due to her upbringing in a large family. She recounts the occasionally "toxic" connection between her parents, which she did not immediately recognize as a young child, which became more apparent as she grew older. Nonetheless, she explained how thrilled she was to find out that she would soon become a mother as she did not expect to become one so soon. She now views the birth of her child as the event in her life that has brought her the most prosperity. However, as a single parent, it is possible that she will need more time off than is allowed which could put her job security in jeopardy. Adjustments on both the individual and society are unavoidable in order to solve this challenge. A mother who has a job values the stimulation that it provides and this is especially true if she is able to successfully juggle her work responsibilities with those of her family. She has to be able to acquire financial independence and the capability to parent a child who she would want to grow up to be an important contributor to society. With the changes in her upbringing compared to that of her child, the relationship between them seemed to change the image of the now parenting style, the emotional linkage as well as the social identity of being a single parent and this becomes an advocate for a different style of parenting as it diffuses the toxicity that is created in abusive environments but still is proof of strain on the parent-child relationship (Putnam, 2006). Current research validates that childhood neglect, emotional abuse, verbal abuse, sexual abuse and physical abuse are connected to the development of an insecure attachment style in both adolescence and adulthood, either through an anxious or avoidant attachment style (Sutton, 2019). Additionally, to her, the identity of a woman is not complete until she has children and a successful career which has in turn made Leyla explain that there is nothing wrong with her "realistic" upbringing.

Leyla narrates that the motivation behind her parenting style is doing the opposite of what her parents did since they failed to tackle situations correctly which in return affected her development. According to Barlow and Coren (2018), parenting practices are a significant predictor of children's outcomes and parenting programs may be an effective strategy to assist parents in achieving the best possible outcomes for their children. Barlow and Coren (2018) also found that parents who participated in parenting programs were more likely to have positive relationships with their children. Leyla believed that children who did not have remarkable parents and who denounced their children's sense of self-confidence had impoverished upbringings. The development of strong, confident and responsible youngsters have stunted as a result of some parenting styles.

In contrast to the findings of Barlow and Coren (2018), Howard et al. (2020) maintains that being a parent is the most essential profession there is. The author believes that youngsters are capable of gaining socialization skills; but, in order for this to occur, children need to participate in formal educational settings. Numerous parents are uncertain about parenting techniques, yet, the presence of contrasting points of view has no bearing on the outcome of this conflict. Others comply with the directive to be strict and consistent by exhibiting behavior that is typically interpreted as severe in the context of the situation. Legislation and recommendations can vary even when they are based on the findings of a study, such as the opinion that councils should be strict against the belief that children should always be permitted to lead and make decisions. Research conclusions often depend on assumptions and not all hypotheses are consistent with one another. This is the case even while there are facts available that support contrasting points of view. Positive reinforcement is recommended, but parents should be aware that it may have negative effects on their children. It is recommended to some parents that they utilize timeouts, however, some parents consider this practice too harsh. Ainsworth, Blehar, Waters and Wall (2015) consider in their 'Strange Situation' study that children who have been ignored or have received a reaction that might have been slow to reach them may view their caregivers as being uncaring or out of reach. If Leyla's parents could have used a positive reinforcement parenting approach, Leyla would not have to go to the extent of having to use the opposite type of parenting style her parents used for her. In one of Ainsworth's (1979) studies, the idea of the caregiver that would exhibit emotions of rejection, anger and that possesses greater restrictions of the way emotions are expressed making the child to be more avoidant was put forth. Children experiencing inadequate parenting may developed the habit of seeking intimacy to help alleviate them from stress and these children develop secondary attachment techniques that they use well into adulthood (Sutton, 2019). This has made Leyla feel like her parents did not raise her well. Hence the reason, she wants to give her son the best, even though she had no plans to have children this soon. Parents should not be very restrictive and overprotective because it affects the children's development as many fail to develop decision-making skills.

Compared to Leyla's parents, who failed to give her space and freedom, she gives her son the space and freedom to make his own decisions, such as choosing where to study and going out to play with his friends. Although Leyla is protective over her son, as every parent is, she is not restrictive. She believes that being restrictive denies a child particular social skills and decision-making freedom, thus impacting their self-confidence and causing unruly behavior among children. Since personality is directly connected to how a child was raised, Lachman et al. (2021) assert that each year, more than one billion children are victims of violent crime, with Asia having the highest prevalence (64 percent). Violation against children is a global public health issue because of the immediate and long-term impact. Child abuse prevention programs and therapies based on positive reinforcement may reduce child abuse. It may also be advantageous to adapt parenting programs to the cultural norms for some countries. The majority of research on the incorporation of parental therapy into conditional cash transfer systems has focused on young children. Conditional cash transfer systems in low and middle-income countries do not evaluate parental interventions. These tactics encourage harmonious parenting and prevent children's behavioral problems. It is because of this that Leyla believes that there is a link between a child's upbringing and personality difficulties, as well as low self-esteem, hopelessness, and physical or sexual abuse, as well as other negative life experiences. Therefore, to successfully give her son the best as a parent, Leyla uses positive reinforcement tactics, a reward-based system, and encourages her son to read more and promote problem-solving skills. Finally, she expresses that this is the best method of parenting because a child needs parental guidance to ensure they make the right decision, however, not an overbearing amount and only provided when needed. Strategies start to become more apparent when the parents show invasive and inconsistent behavior to the extent where the child is not able to gain an understanding of some abilities such as self-regulation; that is seen in controlling forms of parenting (Sutton, 2019). For example, mothers who provided emotional support and guidance to their children have had an elevated level of secure attachment while in contrast, mothers who appeared to be dismissive of their children's emotions had children that show lower levels of secure attachment. These results demonstrate the dyadic nature of attachment and emotional control.

Children need to learn life skills to become competent during adulthood. Therefore, when growing up, they need the necessary support to enable them to know some of these life skills. There are no standard levels of freedom. However, parents are advised to set limits and give their children enough space and freedom to decide what they want (Garcia et al., 2020). Being a supportive parent implies letting the child learn and grow without imposing ideas. Giving them the space needed motivates children in achieving their dreams. However, sometimes, this is not the case. Most parents assume restrictions are important in protecting their children (Banstola, Ogino and Inoue, 2020). Regarding freedom, there are two types of parents, the first being the overprotective parents and the second is the *laissez-faire* parents who prefer giving their children space to learn and grow as they watch from a distance. Two most researched risk factors are maltreatment and violence found in the family that would lead to the emergence of insecure attachment in children (Sutton, 2019). When controlling parenting comes into use, we can also see the emergence of attachment insecurity. This is due to the parents being unpredictable and unreliable when it comes to providing security. Children who are raised by abusive parents may have an insecure attachment style since they regard their parents as unsupportive, unresponsive, dismissive, and hostile (Sutton, 2019).

Leyla's mother fits this description as she provided Leyla with enough space to explore what she wanted in life. According to Leyla, her mother was realistic and had set goals for her, however, her mother also set some limits which were not clearly explained. She recounts that on certain occasions, she failed to connect with her parents because of some unrealistic rules. Like most parents, her parents often worried about their children's future and would want to exert pressure on their children to follow in their footsteps, which is unhealthy. Indeed, Leyla's parents limited her freedom, which according to her, was not a good parenting practice. In the future, Leyla would want to give her children the freedom to decide. However, she admits that setting clear limits like asking for permission for something and also teaching a child the consequences of overstepping these rules is vital (Garcia et al., 2020). This will help her son to act responsibly, especially when he grows up.

Leyla believes that she needs to protect her son, however, she prefers not to be restrictive since this often denies a child opportunities to learn the necessary social skills needed in life. Lack of social skills limits the child's ability to become confident. According to Banstola, Ogino and Inoue (2020), freedom and responsibilities go hand in hand and to make children accountable for their actions, there needs to be clear rules with consequences, to help them make responsible choices in life. A good parent is someone who wants the best for her child. Therefore, there is a dire need to offer assurance and reinforce positive behavior using rewards to encourage children to think independently and become resilient.

STORY 4: ASAD

Asad's character encompasses being caring, adaptable, and affectionate but also selfish when need be. These characteristics can be linked to the culture he was brought up in. Since Asad has had to move back and forth between Kuwait and Canada, his overall characteristics could have been significantly affected, bringing forth the idea of cultural approaches to parenting. Culture plays a major role whereby religion and the overall relationship with community members shape a child's behavior from a young age and prolongs into adulthood (Bornstein, 2012). For example, Asad identifies himself as caring, but a factor could be linked to the type of parenting where culture is the major shaper of behavior. Culture helps shape parents and parenting, whereby, when maintained, it can be transmitted through influencing parents' cognations and shaping the parenting actions (Eyerman, Madigan and Ring, 2017). Cultural difference is further identified in the interview where Asad expresses being more open to staying in Canada than in Kuwait because he feels freer. Children growing up in different cultures often receive specific traits from these environments, therefore, Asad's preference could be due to the issue of Kuwait's conservative and religious nature compared to Canada, where parents can be less severe and traditional. We have seen through statistics that individuals that have shown signs of insecurity have had a difficult time controlling their emotions while people that have exhibited no signs of insecurity have been successful at controlling emotions. Insecure individuals lack mental stability due to their history of stressful situations which makes it hard for them to handle unfortunate life events (Sutton, 2019). The interview helped us identify the role culture plays in different aspects of life and how it also shapes what children think about themselves in the present and in the future. The culture in which children grow up influences their cultural context where they can become competent members of society. Mother caregiving is believed to be the first behavior children learn from a young age, which means that they could adapt their cultural practices easily with their mothers (Barry et al., 2018). Such issues show that, again, culture is the major shaper of behavior and belief; for example, courage, fairness, and caring are what the children should be exposed to from society and their parents. Parents also tend to teach children what they have witnessed within the society based on the culture they have adapted over the years and the teachings that might change with shifting cultures. Additionally, most cultures tend to focus on social interactions and this includes children's interactions with other people and the rules that govern such interactions (Barger et al., 2019). When children are exposed to these rules at an early age, this shapes their self-image and identity. Therefore the culture in which the child grows up will influence their behavior and again, children are more likely to adopt the cultural practices of their parents. For example, parents who are caring and empathetic expose their children to display such behaviors since children will witness these behaviors during social interaction and adopt them with time (Barger et al., 2019).

Trauma can also cause a change in the behavior of a child based on the event and how they can overcome it in the future. Asad, in this case, witnessed a close family member go to prison and this, consequently, created a behavioral change, especially worrying that he might end up in jail as well which is an extremely bothersome factor for a child. The events were traumatizing, a factor that would affect a child's behavior while growing up. The memories of a close family member going to prison affects how the child views the world. Instead of seeing positive aspects in the world, a child could develop a negative view and also develop a negative attitude towards some daily incidents that would progress further into their adulthood (Becker, 2013). At the age of 33, Asad is an adult, yet still, all decisions he might make are based on his childhood experiences, especially the traumatic events that still play a major role in how he will create a foreseeable relationship in the future. Despite the fear of seeing a family member going through such an event, Asad's family were there to guide him on ways in which he could take care of himself and also ways in which he could follow his dreams instead of destroying his life. This interview revolved around the effect of parenting on various children issues which ultimately showed the importance of family bonds which could be an apparent guiding factor. The best parenting approach is to offer parental guidance by being a role model to enable children to make better decisions in life (Barger et al., 2019). However, certain life challenges might affect children's behavior, especially when they experience painful life events like the death of a family member or violation of the law. Certain life events can negatively alter a child's behavior. However, with a strong family bond, children can overcome these traumatic experiences.

So far, we have observed that the parenting experienced as a child to our interviewees is different from what they are offering to their own children. Asad was left to explore his options based on what interested him as a child in order to help shape his own future, which would mean that he would have to come up with the best choices on his own while his parents just offered a little guidance. Leyla, from our previous story, and Asad's parents exercised less Parental Psychological Control (PPC), which meant that the parents had little influence on the psychological reasoning of their children. PPC is mainly a type of negative parenting style in which the parents include tactics such as love and withdrawal to ensure that the children are dependent on them (LaCapra, 2016). In this case, a child cannot make an independent choice without involving a parent, in other words, the parent has total control over the child. Furthermore, PPC has been widely used as a tactic in parenting that would ensure parents can predict adolescent aggressive behavior. Additionally, the approach could prevent a child from clearly understanding the environment in which they live and exploring the overall culture (McNally, 2005). The PPC style tries to maintain the time a child spends with the family rather than with peers, which offers better guidance in real-life events. However, in most cases encompassing peers, children are more likely to affect each other based on the trending behavior and this could encourage them to be more aggressive, a factor that could affect their development negatively.

Now, Asad wants to focus on nurturing his future children by giving them enough options to choose from. However, he still believes that his children will need his input and guidance regarding certain important issues and situations. He also believes that he is in the best position to guide his children to make the best choices with his support.

STORY 5: FAYE

Faye has had support from her parents in her childhood for a very long time which helped her cope with her Attention Deficiency Disorder (ADD) at an early age. Her story has helped us understand parenting tactics' different ways and their importance for children, additionally, how culture plays a major role in children's upbringing. In Faye's case, her parents weren't as strict as other parents around her, allowing her to explore more options in her life than those of her peers. Understanding her environment helped her know that there is more to life than education which shows the different analogies of current parenting. Currently, parents are more concerned about their children's performance and forget that they could have hidden talents that have not been explored due to the fact that they concentrate more on learning. As established, there are different types of parenting and each has different results. The permissive parenting style involves high responsiveness and fewer demands from a parent (Kuppens & Ceulemans, 2019). For example, in Faye's case, she was not good at education, and her parents understood this and decided to demand less from her education-wise. This, consequently, made them concentrate on the other talents that she possesses. This type of parenting mainly involves open communication and this provides a child a chance to decide for themselves when it comes to different issues in the family. In this case, parents can be described as overseers and leaders rather than bosses, allowing children to thrive within their care with less supervision (Hulbert & Anderson, 2018). Additionally, this type of parenting mostly involves fewer rules and will enable children to come up with solutions and ideas that would help them in general. When it comes to rules, they are rarely enforced and allow the children to quickly grow to understand what they are required to do without necessarily being pushed or controlled. It has been argued that permissive parents can enforce morality and self-reliance at an early age, which would mean that children can make concrete decisions while ensuring they make them responsibly and in suitable situations. The parents are mainly interested in their child's happiness at their own expense, a factor that provides a child's understanding of their worth (Eyerman, Madigan and Ring, 2017). Faye was fully supported by her parents, an element that would not be witnessed in most families in her culture, and she was encouraged to take courses that would benefit her in the future or those she was most interested in. In this case, the parents seemed to take a friendship role more than play a parental role to Faye which we will touch upon shortly. Studies show that these strategies occur when parents are assertive and contradictory, and children fail to learn self-regulation skills as they do with controlling parenting (Sutton, 2019).

The death of Faye's father was an event that showed maturity in how she carried herself while at the same time, stepping in to take care of her mother. The tragic event showed the connection they had as a family and how she felt the need to carry the responsibility her father left behind. Culture can be an important factor in influencing responsibility, but most importantly, the shaping of a family ensures that the children are responsible in the future (Eyerman, Madigan and Ring, 2017). In this case, culture could have played a significant role in how Faye expressed her emotions towards her father's death. She invested her feelings in a more productive way in her life (like taking care of her mother) and at the same time concentrated on becoming a successful woman. Faye chose to pursue her passion in music and decided to achieve a Master's degree in Music Therapy in order to help people who are coping with grief and trauma and have undergone the same life experiences as she has. This ultimately showed that Faye grew up in a more collective culture, which brings out the importance of family and the community and how they should work together and look after each other. Individualistic cultures do not necessarily encourage family togetherness and they believe that an individual should not feel responsible for others within the society. Collectiveness ensures that individuals are close in a community, just like in Faye's case.

Trauma at the societal level could be draining, which would mean that people could work as a group within a community to ensure they can overcome them together and distinctly, Faye understood her role in the community after the death of her father. In a collective culture, a loss affects everyone collectively as well, and in return, everyone plays a role in helping those most affected by the traumatic event. Despite her being mentally distressed by her father's death, she also understood her mother needed help, prompting her to take care of her (Eyerman, Madigan and Ring, 2017). The collective culture also allows a child to grow efficiently while asking questions that could be answered easily and building relationships that would help them when it comes to trauma and other life problems. Though collective cultures work in assembling and treating traumatic problems in the adolescent stages, they also create stabilized relationships throughout the individuals' lives (Puntam, 2006). Studies have shown that there are some elements that would benefit individuals and assist in protecting them and in building resilience in case trauma may be experienced. Further research shows the positive caregiver and child relationship as well as larger family systems that impact the extent of social wellness a child displays, as well as the level of flexibility that is shown during experiences of distress or trauma (Chen et al., 2012). Taking a deeper look into understanding the significance of these relationships, this can also have a linkage to the attachment theory.

Depression could be a major risk in the case of trauma within a community, like losing a parent. In this case, Faye could have been at risk of depression after losing her father and taking care of her mother, however, with her free spirit, she had the techniques to understand events and find solutions easily. Parenting, in this case, shows that a child could be resilient when taught that from a young age, a factor that would also help with trauma (Howe & Fearnley, 1999). The parenting techniques, in this case, show much effect, especially because Faye was not neglected, which made her understand the importance of bonding with family. If her father and mother had not registered her academic issue from an early age, she could have suffered the pressure of being forced and compared to perform like her peers throughout her childhood. However, through the care she received, she understood that she was different and her mother was a part of the journey. After her father died, as the leader of the family, she easily formed a bond with her mother and worked to ensure that they could care for each other as a unit. Additionally, the significance of the community in the collective culture played a major role in helping Faye and her mother cope since the support received from family members aided them in overcoming their grief and brought them back up onto their feet; this is only possible due to the eminent support given to them by the community and family around them (Halter and Varcarolis, 2014). Generally, when a family member dies, the family can feel fractured, with children feeling lonely, however, in a collective family, a life event like a funeral is more like a collective experience (Holtorf, 2018). People come together to mourn and offer support. Death in such a situation is considered a crisis moment within a society and society provides a protective layer to help absorb the impact of this shock. The collective culture enabled Faye to see life from a different perspective, hence, enabling her to see the importance of family and the importance of support. It is through a family's aid that children will escape the unfortunate symptoms of loss and find the meaning of life and their purpose. The strong bond formed between family members is what makes the family overcome these traumatic events without experiencing depression or losing themselves to grief.

STORY 6: SUMMER

Summers's personality and her achievements have been shaped by her childhood experiences. Positive childhood experiences can help amplify achievements during adulthood since they enhance the positive growth of the brain and children will start viewing life from a positive angle and attach meaningful perspectives to it (Hernández-Alava & Popli, 2017). Summer, like many children, had wonderful childhood experiences that masked the bad experiences she also witnessed at various stages of her childhood. Her turning point in life began when she started seeing the positive side of life and started discovering her purpose and ultimately, this discovery changed her attitude as she undoubtedly started living a happier life. Understanding one's purpose in life is important in finding direction and gaining advantageous momentum that can help enhance one's journey to success (Wu et al., 2020). Summer had the advantage of understanding her purpose in life earlier than most. Therefore, she did not struggle to find out where she belonged. Understanding one's purpose in life helps plan and focus more energy on something, which helps get good results on time, according to Dam and Hall (2020). However, according to Frosch, Schoppe-Sullivan, and O'Banion (2021), parents are the ones who bring a child to life, take care of them and teach them before passing them to their instructors at school. Hence, parents are an important stakeholder in child-rearing since they handle them during the most delicate moments of their life. Now, despite Summer's parents filing for a divorce when she was young, her mother stood by her and motivated her to see life positively. Like any single mother who is alert of her responsibilities, her mother gave her everything, and her hardworking spirit inspired Summer, giving her hope since she did everything to ensure that she succeeded in achieving her dream career and feeling content in life.

Indeed, as we've established, childhood experiences affect our adulthood and it can be either in a positive or negative way. These early experiences shape our beliefs, values, our own selves and the world around us. Parents play a critical role during this period and similarly, like the foundation of a house, these childhood experiences are more like a life foundation on which our lives are built. If the foundation is not solid enough, it will affect us in adulthood (Albanese, Geller and Russo, 2019). To us, Summer is truly inspiring and the way in which her mother pushed her to work hard by setting rules and motivating her by giving her toys when she passed her exams is valuable. Summer had a memorable childhood due to her mother who influenced and inspired her to become who she is today. A supportive parent like Summer's mother taught her the importance of hard work and supported her by providing her with advice and allowing her to explore what she wanted ranging from hobbies to studies. Again, this category of parenting is closely related to John Bowlby's attachment theory. This theory explains the typical pattern of people, from an early age, that develop and accept close relationships with their "attachment objects," who are often their parents and nurturers. Responding to children's needs to promote both happiness and survival, Bowlby refers to this figure as the "mother figure," which is used to explain why so many parenting stories focus on the mother, keeping in mind that it can also occur in interpersonal relationships (Ainsworth et al., 2015).

Summer acknowledged that she owes her success to her mother because she gave her opportunities to do what she enjoyed, like traveling or indulging her curiosities. Everyone has a childhood story that shaped their life and these stories trigger the old memories which are unique but impactful on their lives (Albanese, Geller and Russo, 2019). Nonetheless, being a single mother is hard. Single mothers shoulder an ample amount of responsibility, ranging from raising their children to single handedly teaching them moral lessons and caring for them at the same time. Most children who do well in life are nurtured and have sensitive, flexible and responsive parents. Summer's mother fits this description because she was admittedly not strict. According to psychology, having a strong parent-child relationship built on everyday moments and positive attention encourages children to become more empowered (Kuppens & Ceulemans, 2019). These children are likely to succeed because they are motivated by their parents and recognize that they possess a support group urging them forward towards success and happiness.

It is not surprising that Summer feels content and happy in life. She has grown up to realize that happiness is something that is acquired over time and not found or created overnight. For her, money cannot buy happiness. Furthermore, Summer notes that success means being secure and comfortable with whatever one does. Thus, successful children are nurtured by parents who are not strict. Hence, parents need to give their children the freedom to explore and make mistakes to learn from in this process (Lowe and Dotterer, 2018). Parents should not be judgmental but encourage children to strive to achieve more and learn. Out of experience, Summer has learned that parents should encourage their children to strive for the better in whatever field they choose to settle in. She expresses that parents need to allow their children freedom in order for the child to make mistakes, but be there to help them stand back up and teach them to learn from these mistakes and not repeat them again.

Having a close relationship with their child allows parents to advise and enable children to learn. However, setting clear rules with reasonable explanations encourages good behavior and also enables children to feel secure and cared for. Not all parents can get a good parenting balance right, and this does not mean that one is a bad parent, it only means that said parent needs to know which parenting style will bring the best out of their children and benefit them more (Kuppens & Ceulemans, 2019). Because of her childhood experiences, Summer has learned some important life lessons and vows not to feel stressed. For her, she will not do anything differently from how her mother raised her. What she *will* avoid is feeling stressed. Summer explained that a journey she took to Bali enlightened her and she consequently became more confident and resilient. Being on a self-discovery journey is the most crucial process in life that makes someone discover their purpose in life (Kuppens & Ceulemans, 2019). By learning Yoga, Summer expressed being able to view the world differently. Summer now sees the positive aspects in life because she has learned to be calm despite facing life's challenges. She appreciates that her mother did everything possible to give her and her siblings the best in life despite working two jobs alongside raising her children. Her mother provided them with the care they needed equally while growing up and made sure she was connected with her children. She created time to foster their relationship and through this connection, children are more comfortable learning and finding their true passion because knowing that they retain a great support system is enough to enable that. Parents need to be friendly but also set appropriate boundaries to nurture good behavior. Children need to live in a comfortable, safe, and encouraging environment created by parents. Being overprotective is a common parenting flaw that pushes children not to adopt positive behavior in order to avoid being scolded by their parents (Lowe and Dotterer, 2018). Strict parents are not connected to their children and consequently, they are not aware of their children's needs. Hence, they miss out on several opportunities to inspire and guide their children to grow and see life positively.

Nonetheless, it is noteworthy to stress parental friendship's negative outcomes since it can also result in unfortunate childhood experiences. As pleasant as it sounds, parents need to be aware of the fact that the repercussions of being excessively friendly to their kids may reduce the authority of a parent to instill discipline into the child (Dam & Hall, 2020). For instance, they may find it hard to punish them considering their friendship level. In addition, being too friendly may allow the children to take advantage of said friendship. Kids may start behaving irresponsibly while knowing that their parents may not act severely towards their actions. As a result, they might end up befriending bad company and losing track of their future. Summer turned out to be an inspiration by utilizing her relationship with her mother to shape her future appropriately. She did not misuse the freedom to engage in irresponsible behavior that would deter her from becoming successful with a still brighter future ahead of her.

STORY 7: NADIM

Nadim's achievement is remarkable, seeing that, at his age, he has an MBA in finance. He is also creative, loves graphic design and calligraphy. He is aware of what he wants in life and has a strong personality. Nadim always believes in standing up for what is right. Personality is important in upholding one's values and ensuring that they treat people and situations based on their behavior or quality. With character, you can focus on the positive side of life and help avoid being stressed by taking sides or confirming biases (Dam & Hall, 2020). Equally, personality helps build strong relationships with people and maintain them. He admits to being a perfectionist, which is one of the weaknesses he openly addresses that affects his work since it consumes a lot of time. He just cannot take anything short of perfection. As a graphic designer, perfection is needed to ensure that customers or service consumers get authentic services which enhance their experience. According to Bowlby (1969), attachment has been described as a lasting psychological connection between people, and is used interchangeably with terms such as affectionate attachment and deep-seated emotional connection to describe the current topic of supportive parenting. Attachment theory includes a child's trust in behavior and a stable foundation for exploring the world freely, as well as a child's ability to seek support, safety and comfort during difficult times. It includes the child's willingness to serve in a safe space and their constant intimacy with caregivers. Despite his weaknesses, he is aware that he is kind, helpful and family oriented. For example, Nadim asserts that the support he received from his mother enabled him to achieve his dreams. Mothers should be passionate about helping their children discover their purpose in life and work towards it in the most positive way possible. They should encourage their children in case of failure and show them the path to success and his mother's treatment towards Nadim helped him find a reason to work hard (Frosch, Schoppe-Sullivan, and O'Banion, 2021).

However, having lost Nadim's older brother, the family felt more connected than they were before, which made him develop a close relationship with his mother. Bringing the family together in case of bereavement is key in enhancing togetherness and mutual consolation. Nadim's mother must have also realized that Nadim needed someone close to him for encouragement and mentorship following the passing of his older brother. Usually, older brothers would act as custodians of their siblings and be responsible for their lives and their track to success. Nadim's mother must have discovered the vacuum left by her oldest son, forcing her to step up and fill his shoes. As a result, Nadim's mother gave him all the support he needed and was always there for him. He was encouraged to work hard to make his mother proud and fulfill his dreams of one day owning a ranch where he could comfortably live with his parents and siblings. This dream has strongly been influenced by how he was brought up. He appreciated the relationship he had with his family while growing up in Saudi Arabia, where they lived together. The close aspect motivated him to do the best for his family. Being a perfectionist, Nadim does not seek to gain more money but a fulfilling life. This explains why he declined to accept a position he felt he was overqualified to accept.

Children always learn and feel motivated to achieve more when they receive the parental support needed to navigate life challenges (Johnstone et al., 2020). Having a strong, loving, and close relationship with their parents enables children to emulate their parents and get advice that motivates them to be their best, wherever they are placed. A positive relationship with a parent allows a child to learn more about the world. They can explore various genres around them without fearing rebuke or punishment from their parents. The positive relationship between a parent and their children would also allow free interaction that provides them with opportunities to be curious and comfortable in exploring. For instance, a child may ask their parents questions about things they have already experienced or things they are yet to experience (Frosch, Schoppe-Sullivan, and O'Banion, 2021). The answers to the questions provide the children with knowledge about their life experiences. Equally, the children may be warned about certain experiences they later avoid for enhanced success and lifetime achievements. Parents who spend more time with their children and create a caring and open environment for dialogue would enable children to be confident and develop a sense of belonging (Johnstone et al., 2020). However, many parents are restrictive; they limit their children's independence, some of them having genuine reasons that they want their children to be safe. However, this limits a child from becoming independent from a young age and consequently, during their adulthood, they fail to explore the world around them and learn to make life choices or learn the techniques of problem-solving.

Some of these life challenges are inevitable. Occasionally, children make bad decisions. However, this is part of growing up and most children, if given the opportunity with the support that they need, will, in time, learn from those mistakes. Psychologists advise parents to start early by giving children leeway but also teach them life skills that they need to survive (Johnstone et al., 2020). Parents are advised to let children experience bad feelings or pain like getting hurt or failing exams for them to do better the next time around. With approached support, children can always do better. Through failure and bad decisions, children can learn that they are capable of overcoming their mistakes, which helps make them see failure as part of life and not a tragedy.

Successful children believe in themselves because their parents believe in them. Nadim notes that parents need to trust their children and also develop good relationships with them. However, parents should always make time for their family as Nadim expressed that since his father is a successful individual, he did not learn much from him since he was never home. Nadim credits his career successes to his mother who was always present and gave him all the support and love he needed. Additionally, his mother taught him to be kind and respectful and these two virtues are necessary in life in order for one to develop confidence and a sense of worth. He also expresses the importance of the hard work he observes from his grandmother, who, despite her age, is still active and does house chores.

Having then lost his father at a younger age, Nadim reveals that he appreciates the family support, especially when his uncle stepped in and became his role model. His uncle motivated him to see the importance of family when he relocated from The United States to Saudi Arabia to take over the family business. Having the strength, especially from family, to overcome life setbacks makes one more assertive and more focused. Furthermore, failure itself should be a motivation that pushes people to stretch beyond their ability. However, family is the indicator of which path a child ends up taking. Children, unquestionably, look at their parents when they first open their eyes in this world and what they see and how they are treated is what they eventually reflect in their adulthood. Early research on different attachment styles hypothesized that caregivers who were more sensitive to their child's needs would produce more secure attachments to their developing child (Ainsworth, 1979).

Nadim's life experiences are an example of how family support can go a long way in inspiring people to succeed. The love and the support during the loss of family members help in the healing process and Nadim is well aware of the importance of lifting each other as a family. The death of his older brother and his father and the support from his mother and uncle influenced him to pursue his dream of buying a ranch where they could live happily, as one. Nadim believes that during difficult times, one needs to be reassured and encouraged to chase their dreams and this requires showing warmth and affection to help children overcome some of the inevitable life challenges.

STORY 8: AYESHA

Ayesha's story is quite inspirational and simultaneously chilling. This story does not only depict a woman who fights for a place in a fast paced world, but also depicts the importance of education and the appreciation of culture in her holistic growth and development regardless of the numerous challenges she goes through (Singh-Manoux & Finkenauer, 2001). Every success is faced with problems that happen naturally to deter its achievement. Problems are like a reminder for every mastermind that nothing comes on a silver plate, that there would be drawbacks, and ours is to persevere and work hard towards achieving our goals in life (Wu et al., 2020). Sometimes, failure may come about. Failure should signal that more energy and resources need to be invested in the same process for enhanced results and not indicate that quitting should be considered. Likewise, Ayesha fundamentally ensures to keep herself moving and further cementing her relevance in society through establishing her own charity group irrespective of being young, only 25 years old. In achieving this, the virtue of humility and consistency is adopted, which also impacts other young people around the society in which she lives. In a nutshell, this brings about the question of the effect of oneself on the people around them as well as the mandate and effort required to change their mindset for the better of their future and society in general (Sue and Sue, 2013). The world around kids brings about various experiences which differ in their extent of influencing the kids. The attitude developed with a particular experience during childhood may be maintained into adulthood (Dam & Hall, 2020). The attitude persists due to the nervous system being familiar with the experience depending on its impact on life. A child who grows up in an environment where the elderly are respected may grow up respecting every adult and doing as instructed, however, a child who has been abused by an adult may maintain a negative attitude towards all adults and consider them bad, thereby avoiding their company and being scared of the presence of adults in their lives (Wu et al., 2020). This brings about the question of one's character as influenced by their behaviors, which in Ayesha's case, is dominated by softness and warm-heartedness. This later helps her establish herself not only as a strong and consistent social worker but also as a lady of the people and for people in general without boundaries or bias. For example, mothers who provide their children with emotional support and guidance have children with high levels of secure attachment, whereas mothers who reject their children's emotions have children with low levels of secure attachment. These results demonstrate the dual nature of attachment and emotion regulation (Sutton, 2019). Attachment is outlined as an enduring connection on a psychological level between two human beings and having an example as above; a mother and a daughter, this bond can be referred to as a "deep-rooted emotional connection," in regards to two caring parents. The theory of attachment entails the child's faith in the attachment figure's behavior and readiness and always having someone familiar to ensure the feeling of safety (Bowlby, 1969).

On the other hand, the role of parenthood in child growth and development in their lives later on is highlighted greatly in Ayesha's story. Early in life, children are mostly innocent and lack the ability to understand their purpose in life (Hernández-Alava & Popli, 2017). Hence, it is up to the mothers, fathers, or adults around them to nurture their talents and enhance their future. They need to be well related to them, give them advice, and ensure they develop positive attitudes, behaviors, and relationships. In Ayesha's case, her mother taught her the value of caring for others fundamentally through donating what she earned to the less privileged in society, which served as a great influence to the prosperity of their wellbeing. Furthermore, we elaborate from this story the importance of contribution to children's education, even those whose association with oneself can be merely depicted through genetics but can be completely noticed through generosity (Tian et al., 2019). This means that Ayesha's mother understood the financial background from which the children emanated and comprehended the importance of education and how it would later impact their lives and society in general. It is through the small things that children learn from adults in their growing process that gets to serve as their key motivational points. Children tend to take cues from their parents and adults in their lives. The adults may hold good leadership positions, are in careers they identify with, or are just impressed by the services they deliver to the community, however, whichever position they hold, children are inspired to follow in the footsteps of the adults to enhance their chances of becoming the figures they emulate (Wu et al., 2020). This can be described as motivation since the child would work hard to achieve their goal. Were it not that Ayesha's mother never tried her best in playing an essential role in the donation and establishment of a charitable organization, Ayesha would never have had the motivation of funding her own organization. Furthermore, due to the harsh environment in which Ayesha grew, she inarguably grew stronger skin day by day which groomed her to endure hardship and to come up with ways of reducing and avoiding said hardship with time and patience.

Another essential aspect of importance in this story is age. It can be noted that Ayesha's story is based on motivation and orientation to hardship in life from a tender age. Nevertheless, her mother is depicted as a woman who fought for her space, that of her daughter Ayesha—and that of other people, especially vulnerable children in society. Ideally, this further motivated Ayesha to understand that being empowered from a tender age is essential as opposed to living a posh and comfortable life, whose sustainability and longevity are never guaranteed. This is juxtaposed with the understanding of the importance of unity and togetherness towards prosperity (Singh-Manoux & Finkenauer, 2001). Ayesha's story shows a clear picture on how children, especially special needs individuals and women suffered in ancient Kuwait, which fostered the establishment of many other organizations who chose to operate collaboratively in order to attain a mutual goal: education and poverty eradication. This brings about the question that everyone should ask them-selves, "in which way can I change the world to be a better place for all?" The story maintains that in most cases, the question goes unanswered by many people whereas few of them work towards achieving the answers—as in the case of Ayesha's mother.

Another aspect of great concern to pick from Ayesha's story is related to mistakes and being successful. For Ayesha, her success was vested in the mis-takes she made, which she learned from, especially after being motivated by her mother. Consequently, many people make mistakes and wind up giving up right away before achieving their goals, which Ayesha radically contests against. For her, it's the numerous mistakes that she had made that allowed her to become who she is today (Shannon et al., 2011). With the support of her parents, she advises other young people to be consistent in what they do and regard the mistakes they make as their stronghold, not a downfall as many often presume. This stems from child curiosity, which if not explored, comes to haunt children later in their lives since it is through the curiosity that better ideas are learned and better norms are cultivated in an individual.

The authors also insist on the contribution of the perception of other people and other social aspects such as language, sports and recreational activities. For Ayesha, those served as her strongholds. Firstly, she expressed that the need to contemplate and consider the negativity on oneself that comes from other people's opinions is unnecessary, rather, the relinquish of said negativ-ity is, in fact, more paramount and essential in individual growth and devel-opment. Secondly, the promiscuousness that emerges from being labeled "different" should be completely avoided. Her story shows that through such behavior, people get to grow up to pursue and achieve a common course for the benefit of all. This is together with being there for each other at all times. As such, it can be concluded that Ayesha's story is strongly directed towards motivating young people towards achieving their dreams and being there for each other like her mother was there for her and how she taught her the importance of caring for underprivileged individuals and minorities.

STORY 9: ZAIN

Zain's story revolves around an individual whose life has been through ups and downs but has ultimately emerged to become successful through setting up various businesses, pursuing a university degree, and establishing a successful family with six children, all spread through various parts of the world. The major idea or rather theme in Zain's story seems to be suffering and success and how the two relate, as well as the factors influencing them or life elements. Of importance too, Zain's story depicts an individual with a sharp memory as opined by Barry et al. (2018) who argues that an individual's autobiographical memory is essential in specifying the extent of their exposure to trauma. As a result, it is true that Zain's memory of trauma is clear and consistent in the story regardless of the fact that at 13 years, he was already oppressed enough in his life and had it rough, especially through his migration to Kuwait, a country he has never been to prior to his move. It is reasonable to assume that people raised by abusive parents have insecure attachment styles because they view their parents as unsupportive, unresponsive, negative, and hostile. A recent meta-analysis of young children found that children who experienced abuse were 80% more likely to have insecure attachment styles than those who did not (Sutton, 2019).

Zain's story shows the attachment he has with his family and the environment in which he grew up in as a child in general. Regarding his life's trauma of witnessing two of his uncle's passing from an accident in Yemen and his pet passing in front of his eyes, it is evidence that even though he was suffering throughout his childhood, he expresses, he does have more to live for. Additionally, as relayed on by Bornstein (2012), it is the duty of parents and guardians to employ a myriad of cultural approaches in parenting to ensure that the children are conversant with their cultures from a tender age. This is exactly what Zain's parents and uncles did, which still remains in his memory even in adulthood. However, the big question in the case at hand is how Zain's childhood trauma has affected his life and how it has helped him positively influence other people in society beginning from his children and other members of his sizable family. In answering this, the story's analysis clearly shows that Zain used his dreams of having a successful business and a good home as a measure of suppressing early exposure to trauma. In other words, it is out of the trauma that the dreams emerged, hence the trauma served as the force behind his premeditated business and family success.

Bornstein (2012) further advised that parenting is an essential and critical aspect that should be handled with ample amount of care as it is a great determinant of how a child perceives life throughout adulthood; the first bit of it when they are young matters greatly. This can be seen in Zain's story as he explains that it is through his parents that he got to understand the source of his curiosity for education and pursuing successful careers such as law and medicine, which he developed love for since childhood. In another research, Finzi et al. (2001) also further associate themselves with the argument stating that parenting approaches are normally passed from a parent to their children, hence using the most appropriate approaches is beneficial for generations to come. This is why Zain argues that his parents brought him up using appropriate approaches, which he also successfully uses in bringing up his children, hence their life, education, and career success. Just like he was being appreciated by his parents, he also appreciates his children and he is proud of them in whatever educational steps they make both in the United Kingdom and the United States.

Relationships and patterns of interaction that are established throughout the early stages of life serve as a model for many interactions later in life and may have consequences that last throughout a person's whole life (Bowlby, 2008). For the reason that young infants lack the verbal skills necessary to articulate their requirements to their caretakers, they often use their actions as a means of conveying this information. Parents often have no idea what their children are experiencing or how those sensations are being represented in their children's minds. Therefore, paying close attention to a child and being in touch with all of their facets is a really challenging endeavor. The goals that parents have for their young children are for them to grow up in a healthy way and to cultivate habits that will enable them to assume responsibility for their own lives. Parents are interested in learning how to be the greatest parents they can be, particularly when they do not desire a simple reiteration of their own unique family history in their children.

To some extent, it can be argued that Zain's consistent talk about the love he has for his children and their educational success is a way of ironing out the trauma he underwent as a child, which he does not want the children to undergo as well. In other words, talking about his children relieves him of the harsh life he grew in as a child and is an act of rewarding and appreciating himself. As echoed by Cohen and Mannarino (2008), trauma focused therapy or undergoing the phase of getting out of trauma is essential for human satisfaction, which Zain does by investing in his children. Were it not for their success, the childhood trauma would still have been affecting him and it would have affected his life negatively.

Zain was able to process his trauma and gain insight into the reasons behind his emotions, actions, and ideas during the course of treatment. Having a better understanding of his experiences enabled him to go from feelings of helplessness to ones of pride. Zain thought that the fact that he could acquire answers for his experiences also served to remind him that he was not the only one who had experienced the things that he had. Recognizing and accepting what someone has gone through is a crucial component of trauma-focused treatment. Counselors with specialized training are able to provide a secure environment free from stigma and judgment in which clients are encouraged to speak freely about their experiences. Those who survive traumatic experiences often report feeling violated as a consequence. The perception of one's own safety is often jeopardized by violations. There are many different ways in which these transgressions might take place, including emotionally, mentally, relationally, and physically. A victim may be assisted in regaining a sense of safety and building a new normal with the assistance of trauma-focused treatment.

Zain's perspective of himself and the world is shaped, in part, by traumatic experiences. Many survivors are affected by triggers in their relationships, as well as in their emotional lives, their physical lives, and their mental states. When it comes to relationships as well as habits, it may be difficult to avoid feeling overwhelmed by the memories and situations that might provoke such feelings. Zain was able to learn and build healthy coping strategies with the use of trauma-focused therapy. It is common for people who have been through traumatic situations to report feelings of shame, despair, and poor self-esteem, all of which may have an effect on how they feel about themselves. Over the course of time, Zain was able to work through his past traumas and reformulate his perspectives towards himself and his children. After enduring traumatic experiences, Zain was able to regain a sense of control over the direction of his life and his family.

Perhaps Zain's good memory is because he was traumatized earlier in his life. As explained by Eyerman, Madigan and Ring (2017), trauma memory is determined by the nature, cause, and severity of trauma an individual suffers. In this case, it is evident that Zain suffered extensive trauma as he keeps regretting the kind of life he grew up in even though he appreciates how his parents and guardians used to treat him. More serious is the issue of immigration, which tormented him. However, his confession that it is through the adventure that he has grown to become the person he is and the teachings of Howe and Fearnley (1999) confirm and argue that attachment therapy is best beneficial when it is done over a long period of time and when the victim is willing to override the disorders that come with childhood trauma. Collectively, Zain serves as a real champion in avoiding all odds to become the person he is today, and he is determined to ensure the success of all people around him, especially the youth.

STORY 10: FATIMA

The uniqueness of the concepts outlined in Fatima's story cannot be alienated. Unlike other stories, Fatima never suffered any issues to do with immigration. Instead, her issues are fully family-oriented, which have caused huge challenges and extensive trauma for her. As noted by Cohen, Mannarino, and Knudsen (2005), parenting should always incorporate the availability and commitment of both parents to reduce causes of sexual abuse and mental instability. In this case, Fatima is mentally unstable due to the effects of not growing up under the full care of her father and having the knowledge that her father later dies from drug abuse overdose. In another research, Cohen and Mannarino (2008) pinpoint that in cases where children grow in a family set-up such as Fatima's, there is often an extensive depiction of trauma-oriented behaviors that, if not taken good care of, might affect or haunt the individuals for life. In some cases, the effects might trickle down to the victims' next generation if similar circumstances prevail.

Fatima's story draws an extensive insight on trauma caused as a result of sexual abuse. Consequently, the fact that her biological father was never available for her when growing up does not summarily conclude that this is her justification of developing a fear of men. A close look into the scenario indicates that her fear and disrespect for men germinates from sexual abuse she experienced during her childhood. Even though her mother got remarried to another man after her biological father's death, the man seemingly used to physically abuse and mistreat her. According to Deblinger et al. (2011), when such cases arise, it is always essential to enroll the child victim in cognitive behavioral therapy to help them regain normal feelings for people of either gender. However, Fatima was never enrolled in any of such programs, a factor that has fostered the continuity and maturity of the thoughts and feelings she currently experiences. Furthermore, in most cases, such programs are often successful when the victims are guided not only by professionals but also by both parents. This was not successful in Fatima's case as she kept remembering her biological father and slowly started losing hope when it became apparent that her stepfather did not understand her thoughts, feelings or respect her as an individual.

Research shows that following the death of a close family member, the bereaved members get over the pain and sorrow after some period of time. However, Engelbrecht and Jobson (2016) counter that the case is never the same in scenarios such as Fatima's. In a nutshell, the pain in Fatima concerning his father never began after his death but rather after both of her parents divorced while knowing that her father was a substance abuser. Correcting such a psychological breakdown might be extremely expensive at times and might cost the victim's life as well. For instance, Fatima completed her undergraduate studies only because her mother was willing and available to continuously support her. However, even with the support, Fatima has not been able to get over the paternal love she missed after her parent's split, and she is not ready to trust any other man apart from her biological father. This situation poses the worry on how she will cope with her love life, including the aspect of having a family of her own as that is a part of the culture in which she grew up. For example, when confronted in a potentially threatening or distressing situation, avoidant attachment personality individuals may use distancing or dissociation techniques to block out their thoughts and feelings and inevitably end or avoid the experience. Theoretically, these methods occur when parents deny and forbid emotional expression without providing examples of effective emotional regulation (Sutton, 2019).

The inability to create and sustain deep, loving relationships, whether they be romantic or platonic, may be one of the most devastating consequences of child sexual abuse. The connections that victims and survivors have, both at the time of the sexual assault and for the rest of their life, are susceptible to being impacted by it. It may be difficult for them to discuss the sexual assault with their spouses, family members, or friends, which prevents others around them from being able to aid or give support. A total of 42 percent of victims and survivors who took part in the Truth Project said that their relationships with other people had been negatively impacted as a result of them having been sexually abused as children.

Abuse of children sexually might make it harder to develop relationships based on trust and intimacy later in life (Fisher et al., 2017). Relationships may trigger flashbacks of sexual abuse in both victims and survivors, and there may be emotional obstacles that make it difficult to discuss the issue of sexual abuse with partners. Many victims and survivors of child sexual abuse find different methods to deal with and react to the trauma they have experienced, and these responses might shift over time (Foster & Hagedorn, 2014). For some people, the psychological damage caused by sexual abuse may be just as severe as, or even more severe than, the physical injuries received as a result of the abuse. Children who have been sexually abused may go through a variety of feelings, including fear, grief, rage, guilt, self-blame, and uncertainty, in the immediate aftermath of the abuse (Foster & Hagedorn, 2014). It is common for victims and survivors to have feelings of humiliation or self-consciousness, and they often do not believe they are qualified or able to discuss what has taken place.

Another aspect of concern in Fatima's story is the effects of the attachment disorder. As discussed by Finzi et al. (2001), there are various attachment styles in which children should be brought up. However, their progress and effectiveness are often hijacked by parental or adult aggression and physical abuse, which Fatima might undergo directly or indirectly after her parents' divorce. Jaberghaderi et al. (2004) prove that there is a great difference regarding how children of either gender behave or react to trauma, especially that which is sexually-oriented. In most cases, boys tend to heal faster and might choose revenge when they are adults whereas girls tend not to forgive or forget easily and have relatively low instances of direct revenge.

Understanding various parenting styles is also essential for the mental wellbeing of children. However, the case is often different in families with a parent or parents who are either disabled or substance abusers, like Fatima's father. Instead of taking care of his family, Fatima's father chose to drink and use drugs. According to Kuppens and Ceulemans (2021), the latter causes parental imbalance. In fact, in a different research, LaCapra (2016) sheds light on how children whose parents are substance abusers and not present suffer more trauma compared to children whose parents are deceased. To some extent, the victim might be thinking that she is one of the reasons as to why the stability, behavior, and even availability of her father was compromised. This might haunt her more especially owing to the fact that he died while they were separated. Hence, Fatima's life might continue being traumatic all throughout if any kind of therapy is still not pursued.

STORY 11: OMAR

Omar is a creative man and a friendly individual but had issues with his parents, who were never there for him. This story shows the type of parenting in which all people living under the same roof appear to be strangers despite loving and caring for their child. In Omar's story, his parents appear to be neglecting their essential parenting role. The neglectful parenting style mainly involves low responsiveness and demandingness, which means the parents are not involved at all in their child's life (Mary et al., 2020). When one considers the outcomes of this method of upbringing for children, it becomes abundantly clear that this approach to parenting is not even close to being optimal. Children need support, warmth, and love, as well as proper discipline, structure, and direction from people in whom they place their trust in in order to be raised to be self-assured individuals who maintain emotional health and resiliency. The children, in this situation however, are mainly strangers to their parents; despite being provided with essentials, they remain in the dark and do not understand anything about their parents. In some extreme circumstances, the children are left to fend for themselves, which affects their growth and development. In such situations, the children affected grow to be insecure and unfriendly because they are used to surviving, which means that they might view other people to be a risk to their means of survival

(Howe & Fearnley, 1999). Omar explains that his father was absent in his life; this parenting style also involves less nurturing, guidance, and attention, which mostly affects the child's self-esteem and personal relationships. The children are vulnerable to underperforming relationships because they have less understanding of people as their ideas are mainly formed through interactions with close family members.

Parents that are not emotionally invested in their children's lives have a low level of participation. They do things for their children like make sure they have food and housing, but other than that, they aren't really active in their life or the lives of their children. The precise level of engagement may vary significantly from case to case. Even while some parents aren't very active in their children's lives, it doesn't mean they don't set fundamental boundaries for their children, such as bedtime or a curfew. Some parents are very neglectful of their children and may even overtly reject them. Children could be provided with the essential necessities for their existence, such as a place to live, food, and clothes, but they might not get much in the way of direction or love from their caregivers. It is essential to keep in mind that the choice to not be active as a parent is not always made on purpose. It may occur for a variety of reasons, some of which include things like having parenting responsibilities and being under a lot of stress.

Parents that demonstrate a style of parenting that is dismissive and uninvolved most often had parents who raised them in a similar manner. They may discover that, even as adults, they continue to act according to the patterns they were brought up with. According to the Child Welfare Information Gateway (2018), some parents who exhibit this style may just be caught up in their busy lives that they find it simpler to adopt a hands-off approach when it comes to interacting with their children since it allows them to feel more in control of the situation. It is possible that some parents are so preoccupied with their own issues (such as being overworked, battling depression, or battling an addiction to substances) that they are unable to see how uninvolved they are with their children or are simply unable to provide the necessary emotional support that their children require. In other cases, parents may be able to see how uninvolved they are with their children but are unable to do anything about it. Omar was raised by parents who were not interested in his life, and as a result, he was left with a long-lasting impression, which he has carried with him into adulthood. It's possible that Omar is worried that he may teach similar behaviors to his own children.

The neglect was the reason why Omar was able to be influenced by different negative behavior such as Marijuana. It is a sad moment that a child has to fight for the attention of their parents and this consequently affects their future relationships. Relationships between a child and a caregiver have a direct impact on the psychosocial development of the child, starting from a very early age (Erikson, 1963, 1968; Erickson and Erikson, 1998; Pittman et al., 2011). The response and attention that the child would get from the primary caregiver determines how the basic trust-versus-mistrust dichotomy is resolved. Children growing up in an observed environment have shown signs to have been able to develop skills that a child from a neglected background could not exhibit. Children neglected at a young age have shown to struggle in areas such as linguistics, morals as well as developing emotional and behavioral issues. The emergence of behavioral issues in later life is notably influenced by many developmental delays, which is linked to neglect (Avdibegovi & Brki, 2020). Neglect leads to trauma among children, an aspect that means that it could affect their academic performance. Cold parenting can also be an aspect of society and culture. In most cases, poverty in some communities significantly affects how involved a parent will be with a child. For example, a parent who is always busy paying for a child's fees could neglect their other responsibilities (Cohen & Mannarino, 2008). In some cultures, education has been seen as the only responsibility that a parent must provide, thus ignoring other important responsibilities such as guiding and disciplining their children. In other cases, the parents do not intentionally neglect their responsibility; in most cases, they think whatever they have offered is enough, which causes major strain in their relationship with their children, like in the case of Omar. However, the disadvantages of such actions could lead to trauma among children and they might grow worried about their societal worth.

Trauma and long-term memory for childhood events affect children's growth and development and mental wellbeing. Children learn that they can't depend on anyone else for support if they don't have a deep, loving connection with their parents or other primary caregivers. As a result of being mistreated and exploited, youngsters develop a negative self-image and come to feel that the world is a dangerous place. The immune system, the brain and neurological system, and the body's stress response mechanisms are all harmed by the effects of trauma on these systems. The story has been clear that neglect had a major negative effect on Omar and how this influenced his initial start of drug use. Compared to past centuries, we believe that in the 21st century, the responsibilities have increased and currently, parents are advised to be more involved in their children's lives. As adults, parents remember the traumatic events that have occurred to them as children and not being able to feel the love from one's parents is a major concern and may affect an individual's memory. Research shows that trauma among children could lead to poor growth and development, whereby they grow into stressed adults and have behavior issues (Deblinger et al., 2011). For example, children could be irresponsible in their actions and that affects how they relate with others, including aggression or verbal abuse. In this case, drug abuse has proven to be a behavioral issue whereby abusers seek a sense of belonging, thus making a wrong decision to fit in with peers. Despite Omar's understanding that his parents love him, he was unsatisfied with how much they were present in his life, which was an issue for him to make any clear decisions and take better care of himself and those close to them. Data also shows that while insecure people struggle to control their emotions, secure people thrive at it. Due to stressful situations and interpersonal histories characterized by rejection and inconsistent behavior, anxious individuals lack the emotional stability to cope with life's adverse events. Problems with alcohol, anxiety, depression, and substance use are also more common among people with insecure attachment styles and have been found to have similar effects on controlled and abusive parenting (Sutton, 2019).

Parenting, in most cases, has been identified as a way of encouraging children to grow to be responsible adults. However, with neglect, children grow to neglect their responsibilities, a factor that could mean they will not care about real-life consequences such as drug abuse. The parental void is a significant issue because it can be filled with substances that make an individual happy. Trauma from neglect could lead to memory loss in children if not addressed which is a factor that would affect the overall learning process of an individual (Engelbrecht & Jobson, 2016). The effect of trauma could be preventing valuable information from linking in the brain, thus causing issues for individuals in remembering images, sounds, and words. Despite Omar having no issues, the trauma is evident through substance use despite not being addicted; it helps prevent the emptiness in his life and this could lead to a more drastic effect in his adulthood (if the effect of substance abuse is not addressed) as a result of childhood trauma. Omar expressed being ready to have a family of his own, but it is unclear whether he will be able to withhold his sadness from his family in the future and if he will be a confident and caring father to his children.

STORY 12: MOE

Moe starts by describing himself as extroverted, imaginative, generous, energetic, and fashionable. As is typical in some Arab parenting, he comes from a background of severe parental abuse. According to Moe, he feels neglected, physically abused, and emotionally blackmailed for academic reasons. Moe states that Arab parents in the middle class are afraid of the future and put this burden on their children, which ends up limiting their levels of creativity, leading to intergenerational problems. The introduction of the story depicts how poor parenting practices have negatively affected the wellbeing of children in Arab countries, including Moe. Dwairy (2004) mentions that the authoritarian, permissive, and authoritative parenting styles are the ones under investigation as potential contributors to the mental health issues experienced by teenagers. It was hypothesized that boys and girls would choose different approaches to parenting; the authoritarian parenting style that is prevalent in authoritarian Arab civilizations would not be related to psychological maladjustment because the psychological adjustment of females and males would be distinct from one another. Furthermore, there is no correlation between authoritarian parenting and psychological maladjustment in children. The results provided evidence to support each of these alternative explanations. According to the findings of a study that compared the approaches to parenting adopted by men and women, females are more likely to exercise authoritarian parenting styles than males. Girls performed noticeably better than boys did on tests measuring identity issues, anxiety disorders, and depression. On the other hand, boys performed far better than girls did on a test that was designed to identify aberrant behavior. There was no correlation found between authoritative parenting styles and indicators of psychological well-being. However, according to Dwairy (2004), there is a significant link between children's psychological well-being and the degree to which their parents exercise authoritarian parenting. In addition to issues like anxiety, phobias, depression, and behavioral issues, boys who were raised with permissive parenting expressed unfavorable opinions toward their parents, poorer self-esteem, and a greater sense of who they were as individuals. This illustrates that different parenting styles are more successful in different cultures and with different genders. It is clear that Moe's parents used permissive parenting practices; hence the reason Moe has negative opinions towards his parents.

When a kid is abused or neglected, it may have long-term or even intergenerational effects on the child's emotional and mental health. Maltreatment of children has been shown to have long-term effects on a child's health, development, and well-being, not to mention the financial toll it has on society as a whole. Some of these effects may be unrelated to one another, while others may be interconnected (Dwairy, 2004). There are a number of ways in which abuse or neglect may harm children, such as stifling their physical growth and causing mental health issues like poor self-esteem, which can then lead to high-risk behaviors like drug misuse. The degree, frequency, and length of the abuse, as well as the nature of the kid's connection with the offender, all influence the result for each individual child, which may range from poor to excellent depending on a variety of circumstances. Other unfavorable experiences (such as parental drug use, marital violence, or poverty) might muddle the consequences of abuse on children, further complicating the analysis (Rosen et al., 2018).

Moe discusses how challenging it is to be gay in the Arab culture, particularly in countries where such behavior is criminalized to the point where it is even punishable by death. According to him, the combination of these overpowering thoughts, his occasional use of pharmaceuticals and smoking marijuana is a recipe for disaster. He also mentioned that he occasionally uses other dangerous substances. In Arab countries, the issue of homosexuality is a debatable topic that has made people with this identity feels inferior since they are underrepresented and harassed. Al-Abbas and Haidder (2020) point out that Arab Muslims are generally opposed to homosexuality. The media often reflects both the people of a culture and the culture itself and the primary objective is to educate people on what's going on in the world at the moment. As a result of the fact that this is its fundamental assumption, it must depict a diverse range of individuals going through a variety of experiences because this is the human condition. In a growing number of geographic areas, homosexuality is not only becoming more common but also more tolerated. In light of this, it is argued that the media should not minimize the presence of people who have this sexual orientation, despite the fact that they only make up a small percentage of the total population. According to Al-Abbas and Haidder (2020), within the context of homosexuality, the media covered six key subject categories, which were as follows: criminal activity, extremist groups, the law, authority figures and scandals, cultures, and countries. According to the findings of the research, there is a greater geographical distribution of nations with anti-homosexuality legislation than there is of countries with a reputation for tolerance towards homosexuality. According to the findings of the study, homosexuals receive an unfavorable portrayal and are underrepresented in media that is produced in Arab countries (Al-Abbas & Haidder, 2020). This has led to Moe developing negative feelings and this, consequently, led him to substance abuse.

As a child, Moe mentions that his parents took their anger out on him and his brothers, and anytime they fought or argued, he was forbidden from going outside or playing with his friends. He felt as though he was constantly surrounded by a ball of negative energy at home. Unfortunately for Moe's parents, they took his academic accomplishments as evidence of how well they had raised him. According to Barlow and Coren (2018), parenting styles are a crucial factor in determining the outcomes that children experience, and parenting programs have the potential to be an efficient means of assisting parents in fostering positive outcomes for their children. This explains the reason Moe is struggling to battle negative childhood experiences that have proved too mentally overwhelming. Parents are urged to raise their children by providing them with support and love and allowing their children to engage in play with others as it is the most important way in which a child can learn to develop his/her social skills. However, Moe never had the chance to build those essential social skills as he was denied the chance to play outside with his peers.

Effective parenting practices will allow children to develop decision-making skills and grow up as responsible people. However, the issue of making decisions for children, such as where to study and what subjects to learn, has proved to be a major problem affecting Moe's decision-making skills since his parents forced him to study subjects he is not good at. This, consequently, has led Moe into developing depression and in turn seeking drugs when he went to study abroad. This was due to the undeniable fact that his parents tempered with his decision-making process since he was a child, giving way to Moe making poor life choices that included engaging in drugs to cope with his negative childhood experiences. According to Bah (2019), as a means of coping with the impacts of childhood trauma, individuals may turn to substances to feel the happiness/joy or the sensation of love that they yearned for in their own childhood or to numb themselves from its absence. In other words, folks turn to substances to experience the happiness/joy or the sensation of affection they desired as children. In order to make peace with what has transpired, it is sometimes necessary to find alternate methods of coping with the aftermath of traumatic childhood events.

The act of parenting directly influences a child's growth and development. The saying that the fruit doesn't fall far from the tree and that the branch grows as the twig develops may both accurately explain the impact of different parenting approaches on the expansion and maturation of children. It is impossible to characterize development using rigid categories since all aspects of it are interconnected. The role of the parent in the growth and development of the kid is one that is responsive, accountable, and unending (Widom et al., 2012).

During the formative years of childhood, children benefit cognitively, socially, and in their ability to solve problems from responsible parenting. A kind and supportive upbringing not only shapes their answers but also enables them to develop into more compassionate adults. Interaction and stimulation are very vital throughout the first few years of a child's life. It is all about being able to identify difficulties, respond appropriately to any circumstance, and acquire the characteristics of discipline, time management, and successful problem-solving via the practice of basic routines at home (Widom et al., 2012). Children see how their parents interact with one another and how disagreements are resolved in the house and they learn a range of important life lessons that get ingrained in them throughout time that are essential for maturation (Widom et al., 2012). With a positive and supportive childhood, a child develops social skills such as getting along with people, working toward a shared objective, having a positive attitude in a team setting, making good friendships, and a great deal more.

Chapter 6

Discussion

The way in which parents enforce certain career paths on children ruins and damages all chances of the child being independent, raising issues with mental health in a society that finds the topic of mental illness a taboo. Children are often left struggling either to pursue their dreams or follow the crowd. In this book we explored reasons why parents might have the longing dreams of their own childhood to be carried out by their own children. It is a long and harsh reality of why many children are burnt out or depressed and their relationship with their parents are often conflictual. Psychological wellness might be interpreted as it can bring about practical weakness (Hayes, 2015). Nonstop mistreatment can change young people's minds in progression and influence development. This research focused on the effects of trauma and memory on the individual's development and mental health later in life, effects it had on their childhood and how that will impact them in their future endeavors. During our time on this research, we have accumulated questions that would help us answer our points and get to know the interviewees on a deeper level; the results have shown a slight correlation between what we have found with our research and the probabilities of it being true. Speaking with the second generation children, the results blew us away, but gave way to a different set of questions altogether; have they experienced their own trauma while their parents worked so hard to prevent it? Has life taken a more natural course of action and still gave these children a couple of life tests on its own? The answer is yes. The results have shown a slight correlation between what we had predicted regarding parents' treatment and trauma, and what research has supported in the last decade. For example, the individuals who have gained negative early life experiences have not repeated the mistakes (or in other words negative behaviors from their own parents), instead, they have used this as some type of tool in order to create an outline to ensure their child is happy, healthy and that translates to success academically, professionally as well as a happier overall childhood experience (Chen, 2012).

As we reflect on our interviewees traumatic experiences in their life that shape and form who they are as individuals, we examine common themes in their stories such as, parents who tried raising children to be close and dependent while struggling to bridge the gap of being from completely different generations (Baby Boomers, Generation X and Millennials). We also explored the link between living abroad alone, and the fear of returning home as they express the trauma of how they can identify themselves with others (Saadi et al., 2021). Perhaps we can connect this to the fact that some parents wanted their children to have a strong bond/connection and to always depend on each other. Due to their own traumas of living alone, and their continued feelings of loneliness, these parents wanted to shield their children from any disconnection they felt growing up.

As we understand trauma in this book, we can see experiences expressed in these individual stories and how these parents could cope with their injured experiences as they comfort and support their children, bringing forth the idea that trauma is dealing with their memories while trying to cope with their day-to-day expectations (Hayes, 2015). Some stories reflect on how, for example, mothers try to be the most supportive to their children as well as a mother figure to others while not having their own "proper" mother figure. These individuals express the need for fulfillment despite the fact that they never felt soothed as children. The ability to create new memories as they became mothers themselves helped replace the traumatic experiences they had endured growing up which ultimately, helped in creating a new and healthier self. Patches of bad experiences can now be replaced with a new sense of a whole new individual.

In other stories, we looked at how death can define individuals as they struggle to create a sense of meaning to their own existence. For example, one of the stories reflected on the death of a brother, and how the grief was a driving force to work hard, continue their respective studies and work on supporting the family in developing independence. In another story, we see how a death of a parent encouraged the interviewee to follow her passion in music and so she went on to get her master's in music therapy to try and help people cope with grief and trauma. These stories yet again reflect how a person's trauma can serve as a driving force to give back to the community, help those that are suffering with mental illness or be a safety zone for those who need support.

We also identified themes across families within and across cultures, for example, although Greece may not be a purely collectivist society, the upbringing of most of our interviewees came from authoritative, controlling, and emotionally rigid parenting. Most of the families expressed tension in the way their parents created stress and lack of support in dealing with such turmoil. Although the families who were born and raised in the Middle East expressed more traumatic memories of emotional and physical neglect experienced in their childhood, regardless of the country, the detachment they felt growing up, seemed to be consistent across culture. Resilience is another common theme that the interviewees seemed to have acquired from having to witness hardship in their childhood. The ability to endure difficulties, to fight for stability and to deal with the unexpected was seen in all of our families. Childhood trauma may have impacted their sense of self and their safety but it has rewarded them with tools that have helped them create successful children. Our families come from different cultures where socio-economic and educational factors may have played a variable in who they are as people but they all had a common goal on how to raise a healthy attached child who will be successful in the society while dealing with their own inner injury.

In summary, the data collected, explored through interviews, is that children who experienced trauma and having managed to overcome their struggles, live a happy and contented life. Whereas some who experienced trauma in their lifetime have continued to let it affect them and they are stuck in the cycle of ongoing negative memories of trauma which controls their everyday activities. The interviews demonstrate that parents who suffered from childhood trauma are determined in raising their kids differently from how they were brought up. These parents wanted to build a close and healthier bond with their children by acknowledging the importance of their own mental health to ensure their children's development was within the norm and free of any cognitive distortions. These parents were protective of their children and avoided any exposure of trauma that was like their experience. However, in our research, we do observe some parents who are raising their kids in a similar way as they were raised, using the same parenting techniques but with some moderation like not restricting them in a punitive or overprotective way. It's insightful to note that the few stories which we see a shift from being overprotective to the concept of "spread your wings and fly," is a new area of exploration. Witnessing both groups of parents, we note the common thread is supporting the emotional growth of their children, supporting their children's dreams, and motivating them to pursue their talents, in contrast to their own parents' motivational techniques. As we explore the effect of trauma on parenting, we are hopeful to see how the new generation of parents are more aware, supportive and cautious on how not to inflict their past traumatic experience on their children.

References

Ainsworth, Mary D. Salter, Mary C. Blehar, Everett Waters, and Sally N. Wall. (2015) "Patterns of attachment: A psychological study of the strange situation." Psychology Press.

Ainsworth, Mary S. "Infant–mother attachment." American psychologist 34, no. 10 (1979): 932. https://doi.org/10.1037/0003–066X.34.10.932

Al-Abbas, Linda S., and Ahmad S. Haider. "The Representation of Homosexuals in Arabic-Language News Outlets." *Equality, Diversity and Inclusion: An International Journal* 40, no.3 (2020): 309–337. https://doi.org/10.1108/EDI-05-2020-0130

Albanese, Ariana M., Gabrielle R. Russo, and Pamela A. Geller. "The Role of Parental Self-Efficacy in Parent and Child Well-Being: A Systematic Review of Associated Outcomes." Child: Care, Health and Development 45, no. 3 (2019): 333–363. https://doi.org/10.1111/cch.12661

Avdibegović, Esmina, and Maja Brkić. "Child neglect-causes and consequences." *Psychiatria Danubina* 32, no. suppl. 3 (2020): 337–342.

Bah, Yahya Muhammed. "Drug Abuse Among Street Children." *COUNS-EDU: The International Journal of Counseling and Education* 4 (1) (2019): 1. https://doi.org/10.23916/0020190416610.

Balgiu, Beatrice Adriana. "Self-Esteem, Personality and Resilience. Study of A Students Emerging Adults Group." *Journal of Educational Sciences and Psychology* 7, no. 1 (2017).

Banstola, Ratna Shila, Tetsuya Ogino, and Sachiko Inoue. "Impact of parents' knowledge about the development of self-esteem in adolescents and their parenting practice on the self-esteem and suicidal behavior of urban high school students in Nepal." *International journal of environmental research and public health* 17, no. 17 (2020): 6039. https://doi.org/10.3390/ijerph17176039

Barger, Michael M., Elizabeth Moorman Kim, Nathan R. Kuncel, and Eva M. Pomerantz. "The Relation Between Parents' Involvement in Children's Schooling and Children's Adjustment: A Meta-Analysis." Psychological Bulletin 145, no. 9 (2019): 855. https://doi.org/10.1037/bul0000201

Barlow, Jane, and Esther Coren. "The Effectiveness Of Parenting Programs: A Review Of Campbell Reviews." Research on Social Work Practice 28, no. 1 (2018): 99–102. https://doi.org/10.1177/1049731517725184

Barry, Tom J., Bert Lenaert, Dirk Hermans, Filip Raes, and James W. Griffith. "Meta-Analysis Of The Association Between Autobiographical Memory Specificity and Exposure To Trauma." *Journal of Traumatic Stress* 31, no. 1 (2018): 35–46. https://doi.org/10.1002/jts.22263

Baumrind, Diana. "Child Care Practices Anteceding Three Patterns of Preschool Behavior." Genetic Psychology Monographs 75, no.1 (1967): 43–88.

Baumrind, Diana. "The discipline controversy revisited." Family relations (1996): 405–414.

Baumrind, Diana. "Patterns of parental authority and adolescent autonomy." New directions for child and adolescent development 2005, no. 108 (2005): 61–69.

Baumrind, Diana. "Current patterns of parental authority." Developmental Psychology, no. 4 (1971):1–103.

Beck, Cheryl Tatano, and Sue Watson. "Impact Of Birth Trauma On Breast-Feeding: A Tale Of Two Pathways." Nursing Research 57, no. 4 (2008): 228–236. doi: 10.1 097/01.NNR.0000313494.87282.90

Becker, Douglas J. "Memory And Trauma As Elements Of Identity In Foreign Policymaking." In Memory and Trauma in International Relations, 73–89. Routledge, 2013.

Bedford, Victoria H. "Memories Of Parental Favoritism And The Quality Of Parent-Child Ties in Adulthood." *Journal of Gerontology* 47, no. 4 (1992): S149-S155. https://doi.org/10.1093/geronj/47.4.S149

Bornstein, Lea, and Marc H. Bornstein. "Parenting Styles And Child Social Development." Encyclopedia on Early Childhood Development. Montreal: Centre Of Excellence for Early Childhood Development and Strategic Knowledge Cluster on Early Child Development (2007).

Bornstein, Marc H. "Cultural Approaches to Parenting." Parenting 12, no. 2–3 (2012): 212–221. https://doi.org/10.1080/15295192.2012.683359

Bowlby, John. (1969). "Attachment and Loss: Vol 1." Attachment (2nd ed.), 470–478. New York: Basic Books.

Bowlby, John. Attachment: Second Edition. London, England: Basic Books, 2008.

Butler-Coyne, Hannah, Dougal Hare, Samantha Walker, Angelika Wieck, and Anja Wittkowski. "Acceptability of a Positive Parenting Programme on a Mother and Baby Unit: Q-Methodology with Staff." *Journal of Child and Family Studies* 26, no. 2 (2017): 623–632. https://doi.org/10.1007/s10826-016-0564-9

Chen, Edith. "Protective Factors For Health Among Low-Socioeconomic-Status Individuals." Current Directions in Psychological Science 21, no. 3 (2012): 189–193. https://doi.org/10.1177/0963721412438710

Chen, Ying., Haines, Jess., Charlton, Brittany M. and VanderWeele, Tyler, J. "Positive Parenting Improves Multiple Aspects of Health and Well-Being in Young Adulthood." Nature Human Behavior 3, no. 7 (2019): 684–691. https://doi.org/10 .1038/s41562-019-0602-x

Child Welfare Information Gateway. "Cycle of Abuse." (2018). (accessed August 9, 2022).

Clond, Morgan. "Emotional Freedom Techniques For Anxiety: A Systematic Review With Meta-Analysis." *The Journal Of Nervous And Mental Disease* 204, no. 5 (2016): 388–395. doi: 10.1097/NMD.0000000000000483

Cockburn, Laura. "Children And Young People Living In Changing Worlds: The Process Of Assessing And Understanding The 'Third Culture Kid.'" School Psychology International 23, no. 4 (2002): 475–485. https://doi.org/10.1177 /0143034302234008

Cohen, Judith A. and Mannarino, Anthony, P. "Trauma-Focused Cognitive Behavioural Therapy For Children And Parents." Child and Adolescent Mental Health 13, no. 4 (2008): 158–162. https://doi.org/10.1111/j.1475-3588.2008.00502.x

Cohen, Judith A., Anthony P. Mannarino, and Kraig Knudsen. "Treating Sexually Abused Children: 1 Year Follow-up of a Randomized Controlled Trial." *Child Abuse & Neglect* 29 (2) (2005): 135–45. https://doi.org/10.1016/j.chiabu.2004.12 .005.

Coyne, Sarah M., Jenny Radesky, Kevin M. Collier, Douglas A. Gentile, Jennifer Ruh Linder, Amy I. Nathanson, Eric E. Rasmussen, Stephanie M. Reich, and Jean Rogers. "Parenting And Digital Media." Pediatrics 140, no. Supplement_2 (2017): S112-S116. https://doi.org/10.1542/peds.2016–1758N

Cuddy, Amy JC, Elizabeth Baily Wolf, Peter Glick, Susan Crotty, Jihye Chong, and Michael I. Norton. "Men As Cultural Ideals: Cultural Values Moderate Gender Stereotype Content." *Journal Of Personality And Social Psychology* 109, no. 4 (2015): 622. https://doi.org/10.1037/pspi0000027

Dam, Kristianna, and Elisabeth OC Hall. "Childhood Experiences Pursue Adulthood For Better And Worse: A Qualitative Study Of Adults' Experiences After Growing Up With A Severely Mentally Ill Parent In A Small-Scale Society." Journal of Research in Nursing 25, no. 6–7 (2020): 579–591. https://doi.org/10.1177 /1744987120942272

Davis, Pamela S., Keith J. Edwards, and Terri S. Watson. "Using Process-Experiential/Emotion-Focused Therapy Techniques For Identity Integration And Resolution Of Grief Among Third Culture Kids." *The Journal of Humanistic Counseling* 54, no. 3 (2015): 170–186 https://doi.org/10.1002/johc.12010.

De Greck, Moritz, Zhenhao Shi, Gang Wang, Xiangyu Zuo, Xuedong Yang, Xiaoying Wang, Georg Northoff, and Shihui Han. "Culture Modulates Brain Activity During Empathy With Anger." NeuroImage 59, no. 3 (2012): 2871–2882. https://doi.org /10.1016/j.neuroimage.2011.09.052

Deblinger, Esther, Anthony P. Mannarino, Judith A. Cohen, Melissa K. Runyon, and Robert A. Steer. "Trauma-Focused Cognitive Behavioral Therapy For Children: Impact Of The Trauma Narrative And Treatment Length." Depression And Anxiety 28, no. 1 (2011): 67–75. https://doi.org/10.1002/da.20744

Dollinger, Stephen J., Frederick TL Leong, and Shawna K. Ulicni. "On Traits And Values: With Special Reference To Openness To Experience." *Journal Of Research In Personality* 30, no. 1 (1996): 23–41. https://doi.org/10.1006/jrpe.1996.0002

Dwairy, Marwan. "Parenting Styles And Mental Health Of Arab Gifted Adolescents." Gifted Child Quarterly 48, no. 4 (2004): 275–286. https://doi.org/10.1177 /001698620404800403

Elliman, David, and Margaret A. Lynch. "The Physical Punishment Of Children." Archives Of Disease In Childhood 83, no. 3 (2000): 196–198. http://dx.doi.org/10 .1136/adc.83.3.196

Engelbrecht, Alberta, and Laura Jobson. "Exploring Trauma Associated Appraisals In Trauma Survivors From Collectivistic Cultures." Springerplus 5, no. 1 (2016): 1–11. https://doi.org/10.1186/s40064-016-3043-2

Erikson, E. H. (1963). Childhood and Society. New York: Norton.

Erikson, E. H. (1968). Identity: Youth and Crisis. Oxford, UK: Norton.

Erikson, Erik H., and Joan M. Erikson. (1998). "The Life Cycle Completed." WW Norton & Company.

Eyerman, Ron, Todd Madigan, and Magnus Ring. "Cultural Trauma, Collective Memory And The Vietnam War." Politička Misao: Časopis Za Politologiju 54, no. 1–2 (2017): 11–31.

Faryadi, Qais. "The Montessori Paradigm of Learning: So What?." Online Submission, Universiti Teknologi Mara Malaysia, 2007.

Felitti, Vincent J., Robert F. Anda, Dale Nordenberg, David F. Williamson, Alison M. Spitz, Valerie Edwards, and James S. Marks. "Relationship of childhood abuse and household dysfunction to many of the leading causes of death in adults: The Adverse Childhood Experiences (ACE) Study." *American journal of preventive medicine* 14, no. 4 (1998): 245–258.

Finzi, Ricky, Anca Ram, Dov Har-Even, Dan Shnit, and Abraham Weizman. "Attachment Styles And Aggression In Physically Abused And Neglected Children." *Journal Of Youth And Adolescence* 30, no. 6 (2001): 769–786. https:// doi.org/10.1023/A:1012237813771

Fisher, Cate, Alexandra Goldsmith, Rachel Hurcombe, and Claire Soares. "The Impacts Of Child Sexual Abuse: A Rapid Evidence Assessment. Independent Inquiry into Child Sex Abuse," 2017.

Follette, Victoria, Kathleen M. Palm, and Adria N. Pearson. "Mindfulness And Trauma: Implications For Treatment." *Journal of Rational-Emotive And Cognitive-Behavior Therapy* 24, no. 1 (2006): 45–61. https://doi.org/10.1007/s10942-006-0025-2

Foster, Jennifer M., and W. Bryce Hagedorn. "Through The Eyes Of The Wounded: A Narrative Analysis Of Children's Sexual Abuse Experiences And Recovery Process." *Journal Of Child Sexual Abuse* 23, no. 5 (2014): 538–557. https://doi.org /10.1080/10538712.2014.918072

Fraser, C., McIntyre, A., & Manby, M. "Exploring the impact of parental drug/alcohol problems on children and parents in a Midlands County in 2005/2006." *British journal of social work*, 39 (5) (2022). https://doi.org/10.1093/bjsw/bcn016

Frosch, Cynthia A., Sarah J. Schoppe-Sullivan, and D. David O'Banion. "Parenting And Child Development: A Relational Health Perspective." *American Journal of Lifestyle Medicine* 15, no. 1 (2021): 45–59. https://doi.org/10.1177 /1559827619849028

Garcia, Oscar F., Maria C. Fuentes, Enrique Gracia, Emilia Serra, and Fernando Garcia. "Parenting Warmth and Strictness Across Three Generations: Parenting Styles and Psychosocial Adjustment." *International Journal of Environmental Research and Public Health* 17, no. 20 (2020): 7487. https://doi.org/10.3390/ijerph17207487

Gavron, Tami, and Ofra Mayseless. "Creating Art Together As A Transformative Process In Parent-Child Relations: The Therapeutic Aspects Of The Joint Painting Procedure." Frontiers In Psychology 9 (2018): 2154. https://doi.org/10.3389/fpsyg.2018.02154

Ginsburg, Golda S., and Phyllis Bronstein. "Family Factors Related To Children's Intrinsic/Extrinsic Motivational Orientation And Academic Performance." Child Development 64, no. 5 (1993): 1461–1474. https://doi.org/10.1111/j.1467–8624.1993.tb02964.x

Gonzalez-DeHass, Alyssa R., Patricia P. Willems, and Marie F. Doan Holbein. "Examining The Relationship Between Parental Involvement And Student Motivation." *Educational Psychology Review* 17, no. 2 (2005): 99–123. https://doi.org/10.1007/s10648-005-3949-7

Goodman, Gail S., Jodi A. Quas, Deborah Goldfarb, Lauren Gonzalves, and Alejandra Gonzalez. "Trauma and Long-Term Memory For Childhood Events: Impact Matters." Child Development Perspectives 13, no. 1 (2019): 3–9. https://doi.org/10.1111/cdep.12307

Green, Stefanie Jill. Meanings and Experiences Of Parent Intuition And Competence. The Florida State University, 2004.

Greenhoot, A. F., & Sun, S. (2014). Trauma and Memory. In P. J. Bauer & R. Fivush (Eds.), The Wiley Handbook on The Development of Children's Memory (pp. 774–803). Wiley Blackwell. https://doi.org/10.1002/9781118597705.ch34

Grolnick, Wendy S., and Melanie Farkas. "Parenting and The Development of Children's Self-Regulation." Handbook Of Parenting 5, no. 2 (2002): 89–110.

Halter, Margaret Jordan, and Elizabeth M. Varcarolis, eds. Varcarolis' Foundations of psychiatric Mental Health Nursing. Elsevier Health Sciences, 2014.

Hawkins, Bryan. "Children's Drawing, Self Expression, Identity and The Imagination." International Journal of Art & Design Education 21, no. 3 (2002): 209–219. https://doi.org/10.1111/1468–5949.00318

Hayes, Shirley. "Trauma And Memory: Healing Through Art." Journal of Art for Life 7, no. 1 (2015).

Hennessey, Beth, Seana Moran, Beth Altringer, and Teresa M. Amabile. "Extrinsic and Intrinsic Motivation." Wiley Encyclopedia of Management 11 (2015): 1–4. DOI:10.1002/9781118785317.weom110098

Hernández-Alava, Mónica, and Gurleen Popli. "Children's Development and Parental Input: Evidence from The UK Millennium Cohort Study." Demography 54, no. 2 (2017): 485–511. https://doi.org/10.1007/s13524-017-0554-6

Hildyard, Kathryn L., and David A. Wolfe. "Child neglect: developmental issues and outcomes." Child abuse & neglect 26, no. 6–7 (2002): 679–695.

Hofmann, Stefan G., M. A. Anu Asnaani, and Devon E. Hinton. "Cultural Aspects in Social Anxiety and Social Anxiety Disorder." Depression and Anxiety 27, no. 12 (2010): 1117–1127. https://doi.org/10.1002/da.20759

Holtorf, Cornelius. "Embracing Change: How Cultural Resilience Is Increased Through Cultural Heritage." World archaeology 50, no. 4 (2018): 639–650. https://doi.org/10.1080/00438243.2018.1510340

Howard, Lauren H., Tracy Riggins, and Amanda L. Woodward. "Learning from Others: The Effects of Agency on Event Memory in Young Children." Child development 91, no. 4 (2020): 1317–1335. https://doi.org/10.1111/cdev.13303

Howe, David, and Sheila Fearnley. "Disorders of Attachment and Attachment Therapy." Adoption & Fostering 23, no. 2 (1999): 19–30. https://doi.org/10.1177%2F030857599902300205

Hulbert, Justin C., and Michael C. Anderson. "What Doesn't Kill You Makes You Stronger: Psychological Trauma and Its Relationship to Enhanced Memory Control." *Journal of Experimental Psychology*: General 147, no. 12 (2018): 1931–1949. https://doi.org/10.1037/xge0000461

Hyson, Marion C., Linda C. Whitehead, and Catherine M. Prudhoe. "Influences On Attitudes Toward Physical Affection Between Adults And Children." Early Childhood Research Quarterly 3, no. 1 (1988): 55–75. https://doi.org/10.1016/0885–2006(88)90029–4

Jaberghaderi, Nasrin, Ricky Greenwald, Allen Rubin, Shahin Oliaee Zand, and Shiva Dolatabadi. "A Comparison of CBT And EMDR For Sexually-Abused Iranian Girls." *Clinical Psychology & Psychotherapy: An International Journal of Theory & Practice* 11, no. 5 (2004): 358–368. https://doi.org/10.1002/cpp.395

Johnstone, Kristy M., Tracey Middleton, Eva Kemps, and Junwen Chen. "A Pilot Investigation of Universal School-Based Prevention Programs for Anxiety and Depression Symptomology In Children: A Randomized Controlled Trial." *Journal of Clinical Psychology* 76, no. 7 (2020): 1193–1216. https://doi.org/10.1002/jclp.22926

Kasasa. "Boomers, Gen X, Gen Y, Gen Z, and Gen A Explained." Accessed August 11, 2022. https://www.kasasa.com/exchange/articles/generations/gen-x-gen-y-gen-z.

Kloep, Marion, and Leo B. Hendry. "Letting Go or Holding On? Parents' Perceptions of Their Relationships with Their Children During Emerging Adulthood." *British Journal of Developmental Psychology* 28, no. 4 (2010): 817–834. https://doi.org/10.1348/026151009X480581

Koestner, Richard, Marie Walker, and Laura Fichman. "Childhood Parenting Experiences and Adult Creativity." *Journal of Research in Personality* 33, no. 1 (1999): 92–107. https://doi.org/10.1006/jrpe.1998.2240

Kotaman, Huseyin. "Freedom and Child Rearing: Critic of Parenting Practices from A New Perspective." *Procedia-Social and Behavioral Sciences* 82 (2013): 39–50. https://doi.org/10.1016/j.sbspro.2013.06.222

Kudo, Franklin T., Jeffrey L. Longhofer, and Jerry E. Floersch. "On the Origins of Early Leadership: The Role of Authoritative Parenting Practices and Mastery

Orientation." *Leadership* 8, no. 4 (2012): 345–375. https://doi.org/10.1177/1742715012439431

Kuppens, Sofie, and Eva Ceulemans. "Parenting styles: A Closer Look at a Well-Known Concept." *Journal of Child and Family Studies* 28, no. 1 (2019): 168–181. https://doi.org/10.1007/s10826-018-1242-x

LaCapra, Dominick. "Trauma, history, memory, identity: What remains?." History and Theory 55, no. 3 (2016): 375–400. https://doi.org/10.1111/hith.10817

Lachman, Jamie M., Liane Peña Alampay, Rosanne M. Jocson, Cecilia Alinea, Bernadette Madrid, Catherine Ward, Judy Hutchings, Bernice Landoy Mamauag, Maria Ana Victoria Felize V. Garilao, and Frances Gardner. "Effectiveness of A Parenting Programme to Reduce Violence In A Cash Transfer System In The Philippines: RCT with Follow-Up." *The Lancet Regional Health-Western Pacific* 17, (2021): 100279. https://doi.org/10.1016/j.lanwpc.2021.100279

Laplante, David P., Alain Brunet, and Suzanne King. "The Effects of Maternal Stress and Illness During Pregnancy on Infant Temperament: Project Ice Storm." *Pediatric Research* 79, no. 1 (2016): 107–113. https://doi.org/10.1038/pr.2015.177

Lautarescu, Alexandra, Michael C. Craig, and Vivette Glover. "Prenatal Stress: Effects on Fetal and Child Brain Development." International Review of Neurobiology 150 (2020): 17–40. https://doi.org/10.1016/bs.irn.2019.11.002

Lefkaditou, Angeliki. "Observations on Race and Racism in Greece." Journal of Anthropological Sciences 95 (2017): 329–338. DOI: 10.4436/JASS.95013.

Lowe, Katie, and Aryn M. Dotterer. "Parental Involvement During the College Transition: A Review and Suggestion for Its Conceptual Definition." *Adolescent Research Review* 3, no. 1 (2018): 29–42. https://doi.org/10.1007/s40894-017-0058-z

Lyons, Minna T., Gayle Brewer, and Emily J. Bethell. "Sex-Specific Effect of Recalled Parenting on Affective and Cognitive Empathy in Adulthood." *Current Psychology* 36, no. 2 (2017): 236–241. https://doi.org/10.1007/s12144-015-9405-z

Maccoby, E. E., and Martin, J. A. (1983). Socialization in the Context of the Family: Parent-Child Interaction. In P. H. Mussen, & E. M. Hetherington (Eds.), Handbook of Child Psychology: Vol. 4. Socialization, Personality, and Social Development (pp. 1–101). New York: Wiley.

Maina, Beatrice W., Boniface Ayanbekongshie Ushie, and Caroline W. Kabiru. "Parent-child Sexual and Reproductive Health Communication Among Very Young Adolescents In Korogocho Informal Settlement in Nairobi, Kenya." *Reproductive Health* 17, no. 1 (2020): 1–14. https://doi.org/10.1186/s12978-020-00938-3

Martí-Vilar, Manuel, Lucas Serrano-Pastor, and Francisco González Sala. "Emotional, Cultural and Cognitive Variables of Prosocial Behavior." *Current Psychology* 38, no. 4 (2019): 912–919. DOI:10.1007/s12144-019-0168-9

Mary, Alison, Jacques Dayan, Giovanni Leone, Charlotte Postel, Florence Fraisse, Carine Malle, Thomas Vallée et al. "Resilience After Trauma: The Role Of Memory Suppression." *Science* 367, no. 6479 (2020): eaay8477. DOI: 10.1126/science.aay8477

Masten, Ann S., and Amy R. Monn. "Child and family resilience: A call for integrated science, practice, and professional training." *Family Relations* 64, no. 1 (2015): 5–21.

McNally, Richard J. "Debunking Myths About Trauma And Memory." *The Canadian Journal of Psychiatry* 50, no. 13 (2005): 817–822. https://doi.org/10.1177/070674370505001302

Milevsky, Avidan, Melissa J. Schlechter, and Moshe Machlev. "Effects of Parenting Style and Involvement in Sibling Conflict on Adolescent Sibling Relationships." *Journal of Social and Personal Relationships* 28, no. 8 (2011): 1130–1148. https://doi.org/10.1177/0265407511406894

Miller, Scott T., Gianna M. Wiggins, and Katherine A. Feather. "Growing Up Globally: Third Culture Kids' Experience with Transition, Identity, And Well-Being." *International Journal for the Advancement of Counselling* 42, no. 4 (2020): 414–423. doi:10.1007/s10447-020-09412-y

Mindell, Jodi A., Avi Sadeh, Robert Kwon, and Daniel YT Goh. "Cross-Cultural Differences in The Sleep of Preschool Children." *Sleep Medicine* 14, no. 12 (2013): 1283–1289. https://doi.org/10.1016/j.sleep.2013.09.002

Mulholland, M, K Robinson, C Fisher and M Pallotta-Chiarolli. "Parent–Child Communication, Sexuality and Intergenerational Conflict in Multicultural and Multifaith Communities." *Sex Education* 21, no.1 (2021): 44–58. https://doi.org/10.1080/14681811.2020.1732336

Muller, Chandra, and David Kerbow. "Parent involvement in The Home, School, and Community." In Parents, their children, and schools, 13–42. Routledge, 2018.

Neitzel, Carin, and Anne Dopkins Stright. "Parenting Behaviours During Child Problem Solving: The Roles of Child Temperament, Mother Education and Personality, And The Problem-Solving Context." *International Journal of Behavioral Development* 28, no. 2 (2004): 166–179. https://doi.org/10.1080/01650250344000370

Nemeroff, Charles B. "Paradise Lost: The Neurobiological and Clinical Consequences Of Child Abuse And Neglect." *Neuron* 89, no. 5 (2016): 892–909. https://doi.org/10.1016/j.neuron.2016.01.019

Nesteruk, Olena, and Loren D. Marks. "Parenting in Immigration: Experiences Of Mothers And Fathers From Eastern Europe Raising Children In The United States." *Journal of Comparative Family Studies* 42, no. 6 (2011): 809–825. https://doi.org/10.3138/jcfs.42.6.809

Olszewski-Kubilius, Paula. "The Role of The Family in Talent Development." In Handbook of Giftedness in Cokhildren,129–147. Springer, Cham, 2018. DOI: 10.1007/978-3-319-77004-8_9

Opre, Adrian, and Dana Opre. "The Gender Stereotype Threat and The Academic Performance of Women's University Teaching Staff." *Journal for the Study of Religions and Ideologies* 5, no. 14 (2010): 41–50.

Osofsky, Joy D. "The Traumatic Effects of Child-Parent Separation and the Importance of the Relationship." Zero to Three 39, no. 1 (2018): 83–87.

Oyetunji, Aderonke, and Prakash Chandra. "Postpartum Stress and Infant Outcome: A Review of Current Literature." *Psychiatry Research* 284 (2020): 112769. https://doi.org/10.1016/j.psychres.2020.112769

Paraskakis, Emmanouil, Thomas Ntouros, Michail Ntokos, Ourania Siavana, Maria Bitsori, and Emmanouil Galanakis. "Siesta and Sleep Patterns in A Sample of Adolescents in Greece." *Pediatrics International* 50, no. 5 (2008): 690–693. https://doi.org/10.1111/j.1442–200X.2008.02632.x

Perry, Bruce D. "Childhood Experience and The Expression of Genetic Potential: What Childhood Neglect Tells Us About Nature and Nurture." *Brain and Mind* 3, no. 1 (2002): 79–100. https://doi.org/10.1023/A:1016557824657

Pittman, Joe F., Margaret K. Keiley, Jennifer L. Kerpelman, and Brian E. Vaughn. "Attachment, identity, and intimacy: Parallels between Bowlby's and Erikson's paradigms." *Journal of Family Theory & Review* 3, no. 1 (2011): 32–46. https://doi.org/10.1111/j.1756-2589.2010.00079.x

Pollock, David C., Ruth E. Van Reken, and Michael V. Pollock. "Third Culture Kids: The Experience of Growing up among Worlds: The Original, Classic Book on TCKs." Hachette UK, 2010.

Putnam, Frank W. "The Impact of Trauma on Child Development." *Juvenile & Family Court Journal* 57, no. 1 (2006): 1–11. https://doi.org/10.1111/j.1755–6988.2006.tb00110.x.

Rajgariah, Ridhi, Smitha Malenahalli Chandrashekarappa, Dr Kirthana Venkatesh Babu, Arun Gopi, Narayana Murthy Mysore Ramaiha, and Jagdish Kumar. "Parenting Stress and Coping Strategies Adopted among Working and Non-Working Mothers and Its Association with Socio-Demographic Variables: A Cross-Sectional Study." Clinical Epidemiology and Global Health (2021): 191–195. https://doi.org/10.1016/j.cegh.2020.08.013.

Rana, Shabbir Ahmad, Akhtar Shazia, and Tahir Muhammad Azam. "Parenting Styles and Social Anxiety among Adolescents." *New Horizons Research Journal* 7, no. 2 (2013): 21–34.

Recto, Pamela, and Janna Lesser. "Adolescent Fathers' Perceptions and Experiences of Fatherhood: A Qualitative Exploration with Hispanic Adolescent Fathers." *Journal of Pediatric Nursing* 58, (2021): 82–87. https://doi.org/10.1016/j.pedn.2020.12.010.

Riser, Diana Katherine. "Parent Trauma History and Parenting Style: Relation to Child Trauma and Child Psychopathology." PhD diss, Virginia Tech, 2009.

Rosen, Abigail L., Elizabeth D. Handley, Dante Cicchetti, and Fred A. Rogosch. "The Impact of Patterns of Trauma Exposure among Low Income Children with and without Histories of Child Maltreatment." Child Abuse & Neglect 80, (2018): 301–311. https://doi.org/10.1016/j.chiabu.2018.04.005.

Russell, Alan, Jacqueline Mize, and Kerry Bissaker. "Parent-child relationships." Blackwell Handbook of Childhood Social Development, 205–222. Blackwell Publishing, 2002

Saadi, Altaf, Kathryn Hampton, Maria Vassimon de Assis, Ranit Mishori, Hajar Habbach, and Rohini J. Haar. "Associations between Memory Loss and Trauma in US Asylum Seekers: A Retrospective Review of Medico-Legal Affidavits." PloS One 16, no. 3 (2021). https://doi.org/10.1371/journal.pone.0247033.

Sabat, Isaac E., Alex P. Lindsey, Eden B. King, and Kristen P. Jones. Understanding and Overcoming Challenges Faced by Working Mothers: A Theoretical and

Empirical Review. In Research Perspectives on Work and the Transition to Motherhood, 9–31. Cham: Springer International Publishing, 2016. https://doi.org/10.1007/978-3-319-41121-7_2

Sabey, Allen K., Amy J. Rauer, Megan L. Haselschwerdt, and Brenda Volling. "Beyond 'Lots of Hugs and Kisses': Expressions of Parental Love from Parents and Their Young Children in Two-Parent, Financially Stable Families." *Family Process* 57, no. 3 (2018): 737–751. https://doi.org/10.1111/famp.12327.

Schnyder, Ulrich, Richard A. Bryant, Anke Ehlers, Edna B. Foa, Aram Hasan, Gladys Mwiti, Christian H. Kristensen, Frank Neuner, Misari Oe, and William Yule. "Culture-Sensitive Psychotraumatology." *European Journal of Psychotraumatology* 7, no. 1 (2016). https://doi.org/10.3402/ejpt.v7.31179.

Shannon, C., K. Douse, C. McCusker, L. Feeney, S. Barrett, and C. Mulholland. "The Association between Childhood Trauma and Memory Functioning in Schizophrenia." *Schizophrenia Bulletin* 37, no. 3 (2011): 531–537. https://doi.org/10.1093/schbul/sbp096

Sharma, Nathasha S. "Exploring the Empathy - Aggression Relationship, and Gender Related Differences in Greek College Students." *Journal of Psychological Research* 3, no. 2 (2021). https://doi.org/10.30564/jpr.v3i2.3124.

Singh, Asha, and Deepa Gupta. "Contexts of Childhood and Play: Exploring Parental Perceptions." *Childhood* 19, no. 2 (2012): 235–50. https://doi.org/10.1177/0907568211413941.

Singh-Manoux, Archana, and Catrin Finkenauer.. "Cultural Variations in Social Sharing of Emotions: An Intercultural Perspective." *Journal of Cross-Cultural Psychology* 32, no. 6 (2001): 647–661. https://doi.org/10.1177/0022022101032006001.

Smetana, Judith G. "Current Research on Parenting Styles, Dimensions, and Beliefs." Current Opinion in Psychology 15 (2017): 19–25. https://doi.org/10.1016/j.copsyc.2017.02.012.

Sue, Derald W. and Sue, David. Counseling the Culturally Diverse: Theory and Practice. 6th ed. New Jersey: John Wiley and Sons Inc (2013)

Suitor, J. Jill, Jori Sechrist, Mari Plikuhn, Seth T. Pardo, Megan Gilligan, and Karl Pillemer. "The Role of Perceived Maternal Favoritism in Sibling Relations in Midlife." *Journal of Marriage and the Family* 71, no. 4 (2009): 1026–1038. https://doi.org/10.1111/j.1741-3737.2009.00650.x.

Sutton, Tara E. "Review of attachment theory: Familial predictors, continuity and change, and intrapersonal and relational outcomes." *Marriage & Family Review* 55, no. 1 (2019): 1–22. https://doi.org/10.1080/01494929.2018.1458001

Teicher, Martin H., and Jacqueline A. Samson. "Annual Research Review: Enduring Neurobiological Effects of Childhood Abuse and Neglect." *Journal of Child Psychology and Psychiatry, and Allied Disciplines* 57, no. 3 (2016): 241–266. https://doi.org/10.1111/jcpp.12507.

Thomasgard, Michael, and W. Peter Metz. "Parental Overprotection Revisited." *Child Psychiatry and Human Development* 24, no. 2 (1993): 67–80. https://doi.org/10.1007/bf02367260.

Tian, Yunlong, Chengfu Yu, Shuang Lin, Junming Lu, Yi Liu, and Wei Zhang. "Parental Psychological Control and Adolescent Aggressive Behavior: Deviant

Peer Affiliation as a Mediator and School Connectedness as a Moderator." Frontiers in Psychology 10 (2019): 358. https://doi.org/10.3389/fpsyg.2019.00358.

Treat, Amy E., Amanda Sheffield Morris, Amy C. Williamson, Jennifer Hays-Grudo, and Debbie Laurin. "Adverse Childhood Experiences, Parenting, and Child Executive Function." *Early Child Development and Care* 189, no. 6 (2019): 926–37. https://doi.org/10.1080/03004430.2017.1353978.

Tsabary, Shefali. The Conscious Parent: Transforming Ourselves, Empowering Our Children. Vancouver, BC, Canada: Namaste Publishing Inc, 2010

Turner, Erlanger A., Megan Chandler, and Robert W. Heffer. "The Influence of Parenting Styles, Achievement Motivation, and Self-Efficacy on Academic Performance in College Students." *Journal of College Student Development* 50, no. 3 (2009): 337–346. https://doi.org/10.1353/csd.0.0073.

Vafaeenejad, Zahra, Fourozan Elyasi, Mahmood Moosazadeh, and Zohreh Shahhosseini. "Psychological Factors Contributing to Parenting Styles: A Systematic Review." F1000Research 7 (2019): 906. https://doi.org/10.12688/f1000research.14978.2.

Van der Kolk, Bessel A. "The Body Keeps the Score: Memory and The Evolving Psychobiology of Posttraumatic Stress." *Harvard Review of Psychiatry* 1, no. 5 (1994): 253–265. DOI: 10.3109/10673229409017088.

Vittrup, Brigitte, Sharla Snider, Katherine K. Rose, and Jacqueline Rippy. "Parental Perceptions of the Role of Media and Technology in Their Young Children's Lives." *Journal of Early Childhood Research* 14, no. 1 (2016): 43–54. https://doi.org/10.1177/1476718x14523749

Waddoups, Anne Bentley, Hirokazu Yoshikawa, and Kendra Strouf. "Developmental Effects of Parent–Child Separation." *Annual Review of Developmental Psychology* 1, no. 1 (2019): 387–410. https://doi.org/10.1146/annurev-devpsych-121318–085142.

Werner, Elizabeth A., Michael M. Myers, William P. Fifer, Bin Cheng, Yixin Fang, Rhiannon Allen, and Catherine Monk. "Prenatal Predictors of Infant Temperament." *Developmental Psychobiology* 49, no. 5 (2007): 474–484. https://doi.org/10.1002/dev.20232.

Widom, Cathy Spatz, Sally J. Czaja, Tyrone Bentley, and Mark S. Johnson. "A Prospective Investigation of Physical Health Outcomes in Abused and Neglected Children: New Findings from a 30-Year Follow-Up." *American Journal of Public Health* 102, no. 6 (2012): 1135–1144. https://doi.org/10.2105/AJPH.2011.300636.

Williams, Paula G., Holly K. Rau, Matthew R. Cribbet, and Heather E. Gunn. "Openness to Experience and Stress Regulation." *Journal of Research in Personality* 43, no. 5 (2009): 777–784. https://doi.org/10.1016/j.jrp.2009.06.003.

Winders, Sarah-Jane, Orlagh Murphy, Kathy Looney, and Gary O'Reilly. "Self-Compassion, Trauma, and Posttraumatic Stress Disorder: A Systematic Review." *Clinical Psychology & Psychotherapy* 27, no. 3 (2020): 300–329. https://doi.org/10.1002/cpp.2429.

Wong, Tracy K. Y., Chiaki Konishi, and Xiaoxue Kong. "Parenting and Prosocial Behaviors: A Meta-analysis." Social Development (Oxford, England) 30, no. 2 (2021): 343–373. https://doi.org/10.1111/sode.12481.

Wood, Jeffrey J., Bryce D. McLeod, Marian Sigman, Wei-Chin Hwang, and Brian C. Chu. "Parenting and Childhood Anxiety: Theory, Empirical Findings, and Future Directions: Parenting and Childhood Anxiety." *Journal of Child Psychology and Psychiatry, and Allied Disciplines* 44, no. 1 (2003): 134–151. https://doi.org/10.1111/1469–7610.00106.

Wu, Xihong, Gang Cheng, Cai Tang, Qunhui Xie, Simin He, Ruotong Li, and Yan."The Effect of Parenting Quality on Child Development at 36–48 Months in China's Urban Area: Evidence from a Birth Cohort Study." *International Journal of Environmental Research and Public Health* 17, no. 23 (2020): 8962. https://doi.org/10.3390/ijerph17238962.

Yusuf, Maulida Shanti, and Chee Chew Sim. " Relationship between Parenting Satisfaction and Parenting Styles of Working Mothers in a University in Malaysia." Psikoislamedia: Jurnal Psikologi 1, no. 2 (2017). https://doi.org/10.22373/psikoislamedia.v1i2.915.

Zervas, Linda J., Sherman, Martin F. "The Relationship Between Perceived Parental Favoritism and Self-Esteem." *The Journal of Genetic Psychology* 155, no.1 (1994): 25–33. https://doi.org/10.1080/00221325.1994.9914755.

Index

159

About The Authors

Juliet Dinkha is a Licensed Clinical Psychologist and an affiliate with the American University of Kuwait. Being in the educational field for over 20 years, her interest has always been in teaching, educating, and disseminating information to the public. She loves to empower Middle Eastern women to find their voice, stand for their beliefs and to develop their identity despite obstacles. Dr. Dinkha has a private practice whereby she provides psychoanalysis/psychotherapy and conducts assessments to a diverse client population both in the Middle East as well as the United States of America.

Nathasha S. Sharma is a South Asian Psychotherapist and ACA Member, trained in Cognitive Behavioral Therapy and approaches such as Mindfulness, Trauma, Attachment, Gestalt, Person Centered, Internal Family Systems and Schema modalities. Ms. Sharma was raised in Kuwait offering her a multi-cultural background. She has a Bachelor's in Psychology from Deree—The American College of Greece and a Masters in Psychology with a concentration in Clinical Psychology and Mental Health Counseling from the Hellenic American University, where she received an award for academic achievement. She is also a Certified Clinical Trauma Profession (CCTP) from the International Trauma Training Institute and Evergreen. She has also completed continuing education training courses in Schema therapy and Internal Family Systems masterclass for complex trauma and PTSD. Ms. Sharma is currently a partner of the bilingual Roots Wellness Center Greece; whose team maintains five venues all over Athens with over 13 years of experience. Her private practice is located in Central Athens, specifically in Zografou. She provides individual and group sessions specifically with a trauma informed approach, as well as training seminars and workshops. She is also a telehealth therapist on several platforms in the Middle East and Greece: DoctorAnyTime Greece, Fitcy Health and JustLife. Additionally, she is also well versed in customer service and training companies to better their interpersonal skills with clients. Finally, she is a published author on the topic of empathy, aggression and cultural influences.

Nourah Al Enezi is a child-life specialist in Kuwait. She earned her BA in Social and Behavioral Sciences in 2022 from the American University of Kuwait. During her time in University Nourah has dedicated her time to both academics and volunteer work, in organizations supporting women's rights and in the field of child development while working with children diagnosed with autism. She was accepted to continue her MA in Psychology in the University of Aston Birmingham.

Ingram Content Group UK Ltd.
Milton Keynes UK
UKHW010618010523
421006UK00003B/17

9 781666 925074